Here's wh

When ⌣⌣⌣ ⌣⌣⌣⌣

"I started reading this book and couldn't stop. It is a 'must read' for anyone who wants to know more of how God works in this world bringing light to dark places. This book is a compelling testimony of God's power in the lives of the Chipaya believers who trusted him against impossible odds." – *Bernie May, former President of JAARS and President of Wycliffe USA*

"Most of us who have our Bibles do not realize the perseverance and patience involved in a Bible translation project with a group of people that initially had little or no interest in such a venture. Fran's story of their translation work with the Chipaya of Bolivia documents how language and culture learning were the foundation for their ministry of community support; including medical and practical assistance for the people. Fran recalls the courageous and sometimes frightening trips to the 12,000' village area and the degree of superstition, fear and drunken rituals that greeted them. Years later a church was established and it has endured, despite early persecution and problems. After seventeen years the New Testament was completed. Fran outlines in detail these stories and more in a book that will challenge you to thank God for the Bible in your own language." – *Karl Franklin, Ph.D., International Anthropology Consultant for the Summer Institute of Linguistics*

"As an eye witness from day one and a participant in the Chipaya New Testament dedication seventeen years later, I was amazed to see the changes in Chipaya; a tribute to the power of God to change individuals and their community." – *Dave Farah, a colleague in Bolivia*

"As of 2009, Wycliffe Bible Translators have helped translate 735 New Testaments and 24 complete Bibles, and are working in 1363 languages worldwide. Some language groups have tens of millions of speakers while others have less than one hundred. There were barely 850 Chipaya speakers when the Olsons arrived in 1961. They number about 2500 today. Each situation has its unique set of challenges, joys and sorrows, but everyone deserves a chance to hear God speak to them in their heart language. After all, the angels told the shepherds that the good news of a Savior being born was *for all people.* There are still 2,252 language groups waiting to hear God's voice. Might one of them be waiting for *you?*" – *Bryan Harmelink, Wycliffe International*

WHEN GOD CAME TO TOWN

Published by:
Intermedia Publishing Group, Inc.
P.O. Box 2825
Peoria, Arizona 85380
www.intermediapub.com

ISBN 978-1-935529-71-2

WHEN GOD CAME TO TOWN

By Fran Halterman

Fran Halterman
Psalm 66:5

Intermedia Publishing Group

CONTENTS

THIS BOOK IS DEDICATED TO:

The memory of my husband, Ron Olson, a godly, loving and wise husband and father as well as an excellent linguist and Bible translator.

And to Maximo and other Chipaya believers who were willing to suffer for *entering God's Way* rather than go back to *the old ways*.

ACKNOWLEDGEMENTS

First of all I thank God for the privilege of living in Chipaya and witnessing his unforgettable deeds. I've written this book because in Psalm 115:1 it says, "Let the whole world know what he has done. Tell everyone about his miracles." So I invite you to "Come and see what our God has done" – in Chipaya. (Ps. 66:5)

I'm thankful for my husband, Ron Olson, who poured his heart and soul and energy into giving God's Word to the Chipaya people and loved them till he died in 2003; and I'm thankful for my daughters, Debbie, Carla, Barbie and Amy, who added love and laughter to village living.

But Ron and I could not have translated the New Testament alone, so I say thanks to:

My family, friends and churches in the U.S. who supported us financially and with their prayers from the day we arrived in Chipaya until today, almost fifty years later!

To the pilots, radio technicians, nurses, teachers, administrators, typists, printers, and all our other colleagues who were always ready to extend a helping hand. You will meet a few of them in these pages but many more were serving behind the scenes.

To numerous dear friends who have encouraged me over the years to share the Chipaya Story and "Tell the world about his unforgettable deeds" (Ps. 9:11).

To David and Margaret Bendor-Samuel who for years have been asking, "How's it coming?"

iv

To Terry Whalin who insisted, "You can do it!"

To Majetta Morris, a freelance editor who helped me organize and tighten up the manuscript.

And last but not least to my husband, Vick Halterman, who has encouraged me to keep at it, and has rescued me countless times from computer glitches and witches!

May this story reassure you of God's love and power to make us his children and transform us by his presence in our lives.

FOREWORD

Of the 6,000+ languages in the world today, less than half have a Bible. Ron and Fran Olson's goal, as members of Wycliffe Bible Translators (WBT), was to introduce Jesus, the Son of God, to one of these groups. How? By living among them and translating the New Testament and some Old Testament background material so the people could know and worship God and form their own church. But first the Olsons had to learn and analyze the grammar of the language, make an alphabet, and teach the people to read and write their language.

Six years earlier, the Bolivian government had invited the Summer Institute of Linguistics (SIL), a scientific and educational organization, to transcribe the languages of its minority groups and teach the people to read and write. Since the government was happy for SIL, a sister organization of WBT, to also translate and teach the Bible, the Olsons accepted the challenge.

When they arrived in Bolivia in January, 1961, linguist-translators were already learning several lowland languages. Two different couples had gone to Chipaya, a small town in the highlands, but had had to leave for various reasons.

The mission director asked the Olsons, "Which language group would you like to live with?"

Ron asked, "Which is neediest?"

When the director answered, "Chipaya," Ron said, "Then we'll go to Chipaya."

The following is the story of the next seventeen years, culminating with the dedication of the Chipaya New Testament on Easter Sunday, 1978.

Chipaya refers to the town, the language and the people who speak the language.

After translating the Chipaya New Testament, Ron and a Quechua pastor translated the New Testament into the North Bolivia Quechua language. Although Ron also served as a consultant to other linguist-translators and held various administrative positions, the Chipayas always held a special place in his heart. In the summer of 2003, Ron's wife and daughters stood around his bed singing Chipaya hymns as they waited for God to welcome him home to Heaven.

INTRODUCTION

The picturesque Chipayas are remnants of a mysterious past. Centuries before the rise of the Inca Empire their ancestors dominated the Bolivian highlands, but their language seems to indicate they are related to the Maya people of Mexico and Guatemala.

In their ancient way of life they hunted water birds with bolas and fished with unusual straw scoops. As the marshes dried up and fish became scarce, the men began herding sheep and llamas and raising quinoa, the only crop that grows in their sandy, salty soil.

Life for many generations has been a twofold struggle – to eke out an existence from the salty soil and to appease all the spirits which could harm them. Ancestor spirits, nature spirits, saints and demons required countless animal sacrifices which kept all of the people poor.

When the Incas, Aymaras and Spaniards came, the Chipayas chose to retreat into No-Man's-Land rather than be dominated. In their language, *escape* and *win* are the same word. In this way they preserved their freedom and lifestyle, their language, their dress and hairstyle. They were proud to be Chipaya, proud to be free – not realizing they were slaves to a multitude of evil spirits.

The world, except for a few anthropologists, passed them by.

1

LIFE IN CHIPAYA
BEFORE GOD CAME
1960

FREE TO WORSHIP?

The drumbeat quickened to a loud crescendo then stopped short. Carlos leaned against the adobe wall, dropping his sticks in the cold sand. His fingers were numb. So were his sandaled feet. Even through his thick wool poncho, he felt the icy fingers of wind that swept across the barren plains. In the thin gray dawn he could barely distinguish his Chipaya companions – men in homespun tunics and trousers; women in dark dresses with babies on their backs.

Carlos was proud to be a Chipaya, for they had never been conquered, not even by the Incas. They had always managed to escape and be free – free to live and worship as they pleased. Carlos reached into his pouch for another wad of coca leaves, hoping they would lessen the cold and dull ache in his head. They had been dancing and drinking all night and must continue all day till sundown. How else could they pacify the river spirit and be assured of a good quinoa crop? Two years ago when the river was low the sun parched their quinoa grain, and last year it washed their crops away. They couldn't take another lean year!

Carlos fished inside his tunic for a tiny aluminum cup as the fiesta leader made the rounds, pouring watered down alcohol from a grimy little teapot. A good leader filled their cups often.

After they had all drunk and rested a bit, Carlos picked up his sticks and started the rhythm again. One by one, wooden flutes and panpipes joined in. Mechanically the men and women rose and half danced, half marched around the open plaza, which separated the two sides of town, then wound their way between clusters of little round huts.

Finally the sun crept over the horizon, chasing away the shadows. They stopped for another drink, grateful that the long cold night was over. Carlos looked around the group of dancers. Every Chipaya used to join in the rituals till some foreigners came to live among them. They brought medicines, wrote down their words, and taught about a God Who was greater than the spirits they worshipped. The medicines were all right, but now some of the people had left the old way to serve this *new* God.

Take Ceferino, for example; he used to drink to the spirits at every fiesta. Now he refused to take part at all, saying he was free to worship whoever he chose, and now he worshipped the *true* God. Of course he was free: they all were. But how could he be a true Chipaya and not worship the spirits? Besides, it was unfair not to help appease them – and it could be dangerous, too.

Just then Ceferino hurried by on his way to the village well. Carlos stopped him and threw an arm around his shoulder, breathing in his face. "Ceferino, brother, drink with us to the river spirit," he urged, pressing his little cup of alcohol to Ceferino's lips.

But Ceferino shook his head. "No, brother. I've entered God's Way and worship only Him. You should follow Him too, Carlos. He's a good God. The old ways always end badly. You know they do."

Carlos turned away, muttering to himself. It wasn't his fault people picked fights with him when he was drunk.

Now other men crowded around Ceferino, offering their drinks in a friendly way at first, but growing angry when he refused them. Finally he managed to break away.

Disgruntled, the crowd continued drinking and dancing. Before long Carlos' poncho felt hot and heavy. He was relieved at last to stop at the fiesta leader's house. He was glad it wasn't his animals that would be sacrificed for the community meal. He joined the men who formed a circle around a llama, a pig and a sheep and helped sprinkle coca leaves and alcohol on them. Then, bleary-eyed and groggy, he sagged against the house and dozed till the pig's squeals roused him. Now they were pouring blood on the ground for the river spirit. Would the sacrifices pacify him for another year? Only time would tell.

The rituals completed, Carlos reluctantly started drumming again. As the hours dragged by, his thoughts kept turning to Ceferino. Who ever heard of worshiping a good God? If he didn't eat your child's spirit or ruin your crops, why worry about Him? His wife wished he'd quit fighting and going off with other women at all the fiestas, but if he didn't drink, the spirits would be offended and his friends would despise him – like they despised Ceferino! No, that was too much to ask. God's Way might be good, but it wasn't for him. Maybe someday. After all, he was free to worship whom he chose.

As the blazing sun beat down, the group dwindles. His head was pounding. The music was muddled, the dancers sluggish. Why were the spirits so hard to please?

It seemed like an eternity before the fiery sun sank toward the distant mountains, signaling time for the sacrificial meal. Now crowds gathered from all over the village for the free food – piles of steamed quinoa meal and five-gallon cans of quinoa soup. Carlos drank two big bowlfuls of soup, devoured a hatful of fluffy quinoa and boiled corn, then chewed on the tough meat. For awhile the food and cool shade helped him forget the throbbing in his head.

As soon as the sun disappeared, the chill crept back across the barren plains. Again his poncho felt good. The food was gone. The fiesta was over. Some folks were staggering home, supporting each other. Little children tugged at their mother's skirts, begging them to come home. Carlos' wife pulled at his poncho, pleading, "Please come home before you get in trouble!" But how could he leave now? The fiesta leader was still supplying drinks! He pushed her away and crowded into the small round hut with other men and women, slouching on the sheepskins that carpeted the dirt floor. By flickering candlelight they continued drinking. There was hoarse laughter. Arguing. More drinking.

Finally Carlos had had enough. He edged closer to the woman next to him and said, "Let's go." She eyed him scornfully and turned away.

"I say, let's go!" he insisted, grabbing her arm.

She pulled away and slapped his face, muttering, "Leave me alone."

No one was going to treat him like that! Enraged, he felt around on the dark floor till his hand found a bottle. He clutched it and swung, breaking it over her head. She screamed, but he swung again. With a moan she slumped over, blood streaming down her face.

Then terror gripped Carlos. What if he had killed her? What would her husband do to him? Why did fiestas always end this way? His companions crowded around, yanking at him and shouting. Desperately he jerked away and escaped into the blackness. The fresh air and cold wind in his face helped him think. The foreigner – Tall Brother – maybe he could help! Blindly he stumbled across the dark plaza. Yes, Ceferino was right. These ways always ended badly. He had had enough.

Reaching the foreigner's house, he banged on the door till it opened, then stumbling into the room he fell on his knees before the Bible translator, sobbing, "Tall Brother, please help me!"

Tall Brother pulled him to his feet, saying, "Don't kneel to me. I'm just a man. What's wrong?"

"It's Viviana – her head – it's bleeding. Please come!"

Tall Brother was already reaching for bandages and medicines and lifting the kerosene lantern off its hook.

As the two men hurried back across the plaza Carlos was still sobbing. "The old ways – they're no good. I've had enough of them. I'm going to enter God's Way, like Ceferino. Really I am, Brother – tomorrow – when I'm sober – tomorrow – I really am…"

But tomorrow came and went and Carlos just couldn't make the break. The deep gash in Viviana's forehead began to heal. Her husband demanded several precious sheep in payment, but the community soon forgot the incident, as fights were common during fiestas. The weeks passed. More fiestas came. Carlos didn't want to take part, but how could he offend the spirits? And how could he refuse to drink with his friends? Again he drank. Again he fought.

At last he realized he wasn't free – he was a slave![1]

2

SETTLING IN
1961-1962

THE FIRST THREE MONTHS

First You Have to Get There

When Ron Olson and Dave Farah reached the Chipaya village in early August, 1961, Ron told the people, "My wife and I would like to learn your language, write it down, teach you to read, and translate the Bible and other good books for you. May we live here?" They were actually the third visitors to make that speech. About four years earlier, the Chipayas had eyed the first American couple suspiciously, discussed the matter and said, "No. There's no place." No place? The barren plateau stretched to the horizon in all directions. Consequently, the couple settled in Escara, a near-by town, to try to make friends and learn the language. A couple years later, however, they had to leave for medical reasons.

The second couple was allowed to live in town, but only stayed a few months before returning to the U.S., leaving their Army surplus Jeep for whoever came next.

Two years later, in 1961, Ron and I accepted the challenge, but first Ron had to resurrect the Jeep. He replaced the front axle, rings and valves; ground the bearing inserts to the right size, soldered the gas line, patched the tires, and finally found the right size nuts for the wheel hubs. Then he packed a few clothes and household items, and tied a couple of empty barrels on the Jeep roof. When all was ready, we huddled in the street while a co-worker prayed, "Please protect them, dear God, and help the Chipayas learn to know and worship you."

Then Ron and Dave, a colleague, drove out of the Cochabamba valley and over the towering Andes Mountains to Oruro, a city on the *altiplano* (high plateau) at 12,000 feet altitude. The next morning they bought a few supplies, introduced themselves to the Director of Rural Education who wrote a letter of introduction to local school directors, then headed southwest across the plains. (See the map on page 2 of the photo section.)

For two days Ron and Dave followed telegraph poles, truck tracks or llama trails through sand and rivers, at times wending their way through miles of low shrubs. At each small town they introduced themselves to the local authority, since few foreigners traveled that way.

The evening of the second day, after safely fording the wide Lauca River, they reached Escara, the last Aymara town before Chipaya. The school director offered them lodging after reading the letter from his boss in Oruro. In the morning Ron said, "Thanks for everything. We'll be on our way now."

But their host said, "You have to cross another branch of the Lauca River, and you can't do that till the ice melts!"

"What time will that be?"

"About noon."

"Not till noon?!"

"That's right." Being south of the equator, August was mid-winter.

Finally, after lunch, they headed for Chipaya. Half an hour later they reached the second branch of the Lauca River. They waded across, checking for deep spots, then drove across. Now the land was really bare – no shrubs or straw – just a little grass and a sort of tundra landscape.

When they finally drove into the village of Chipaya, they made the speech about living there to learn the language, put it in writing and translate the Bible.

The Chipayas recognized the Jeep and said, "Yes! And we'll build you a house if you bring the doors, windows and roof poles, then you can live in it as long as you like and when you leave, it will be a community house. When will you come?" Amazed by their generosity, Ron said, "I'll be back in a week with my wife and baby."

Road to our New Home

A week later, Dave accompanied Ron and me as we left civilization behind and lumbered through sand and ruts and rivers for ten hours, stopping only to clean sand out of the brakes. Debbie, two and a half months old, was doing great. About six o'clock we reached the first branch of the Lauca River, thankful to be nearing Escara before dark. All was going well until we sank into the spongy sand in the middle of the wide river! The motor quit. We all groaned. Now what?!

We decided Dave should stay with the Jeep while Ron and I walked to town. We took off our shoes and stepped into the icy cold water, carrying Debbie in a cocoon of blankets. After putting on our shoes, we started walking quickly. It was getting dark, windy and cold, but at least we could see the road. In no time we were panting and remembered we were at 12,000 feet! An hour later we finally dragged into Escara and knocked on the school director's door.

Ron said, "The Jeep is stuck in the middle of the river! Could you help us?"

He said, "I'll take you to a truck owner who can pull you out."

By then, Debbie was hungry and crying. I mixed a bottle of milk, but she wouldn't drink it cold and just kept crying. It had been a very long day and I was exhausted. I looked around the bedroom, desperate for a way to warm her bottle. Seeing the kerosene pressure lamp hanging from a rafter, I held Debbie in one arm, and stood on tiptoes to hold her bottle in the heat above the lamp. Suddenly the glass bottle burst, spilling milk over the hot metal lampshade and down on us. That was the last straw, and I burst into tears. Fortunately, Ron saved the day by finding another bottle in the diaper bag and warming it in the kitchen.

Ron's next challenge was to convince the truck owner and a crew of Aymara Indians to rescue the Jeep. They said, "We'll do it tomorrow."

Ron said, "Tomorrow will be too late. The motor will be full of sand!"

When he raised their wages they finally agreed, asking, "Do you have a rope?"

Ron said, "Yes."

When they saw our nylon rope, they were incredulous. "*That* thin thing?"

"It's very strong."

"Are you *sure?*"

Ron laughed, "I'm sure." It was 1000 pound test nylon rope, one of our unique wedding gifts as we planned to go overseas!

The river was so cold, Ron's feet were numb and aching in a few minutes. He wondered how the Aymara men stood it for an hour and a half. By the time they finally pulled the Jeep out, the river was beginning to freeze over.

The next day, August 6, was Bolivia's Independence Day. School children marched and sang and dignitaries made speeches. Finally, after a community meal, we headed for Chipaya.

Leaving Escara, we crossed the second branch of the Lauca River. Now the plains stretched out in all directions, with snow-covered peaks of the Andes to the far west, marking the border with Chile.

Sandy stretches sparkled in the bright sun. A few sheep and llamas grazed in green areas near the river and in the distance stood little clusters of cone-shaped structures. "Those are the Chipayas' country homes, near their flocks," Ron said. Straight ahead, a tiny white tower floated in a shimmering sea. "And that's the bell tower in Chipaya. We're getting close now!" My heart was pounding. We were finally approaching our destination! I'd always dreamed of being a missionary where people hadn't heard of Jesus – and finally my dream was coming true!

Another mile or two and the shimmering sea disappeared, leaving the tower on dry ground. I strained my eyes to see more. In a few minutes little houses appeared near the tower, but I couldn't see any church.

Finally, driving into town, we passed the bell tower and stopped in the big empty plaza. So this was Chipaya – our new home! Clusters of round houses with straw roofs stood on either side of the plaza. Since all the doors faced east, those on our right faced the plaza while those on our left had no doors in view.

For ten minutes, we were trapped in the Jeep by a crowd of men shaking grimy hands through the windows. Their welcome overwhelmed us. They all looked alike. I wondered, "How will I ever tell them apart?"

First Impressions
The People

The men were dark skinned, about five feet, six or eight inches tall. They wore striped tunics tied with a braided cord at the waist, over white shirts and dark trousers, all of homespun wool. Colorful earflaps showed beneath white felted hats. They also had brightly colored squares that looked like hot pads tucked into their belts! Some wore truck-tire sandals while others were barefoot. Boys dressed like the men, minus the white felt hats, showing off their knitted caps. A young man named Ceferino was very friendly. He said he knew the two couples who had preceded us.

The women wore dark homespun dresses over white blouses with long blue sleeves. Their dresses were gathered with a wide belt at the waist and pinned at the shoulders with three-inch safety pins connected to a silver chain. Safety pins of various sizes adorned their blouses. All the women and girls had their hair parted in the middle, with a tight row of tiny braids on either side of the part. Their long, tiny braids were plaited into two long braids hanging down their backs.

Young men came around to converse in Spanish but women and small children peeked from behind the houses. When I walked over to greet them, they just said, "No se. No se." (I don't know.) I was glad when a lady came by later, smiled at Debbie and said, "*Anchacacha....*" I grabbed paper and a pencil and tried to write it down. It sounded like one long word with lots of *a*'s. She repeated it a couple times then said something else and hurried away. I thought, "Oh boy! What a language! Will I ever learn it?" Later, with help, we deciphered my scribbles: "*Ancha c'achalya am wawalya*," meaning "Your baby is very nice." It just happened that all the vowels were *a*'s.

The school children were more curious than timid. Within a few days they were running to our house during recess to see baby Debbie and tell me the names of things. They showed me where to draw water from shallow wells around town, with a tin can on a short rope – and how to drop the can so it would fill with water. Soon they were begging to bring a pail of water to earn a piece of hard candy.

Our little neighbor, Mateo, was full of mischief. When Ron noticed that wires in the Jeep motor had been pulled loose, school boys whispered that Mateo had done it. He didn't know they told us, and thought maybe the radio had!

The Houses

The round town houses were made of sod blocks, cut to form a circle, and always placed upside down. The rafters were two series of hoops, or arches, formed by tying small shrubs together with straw rope. Over the hoops they laid a mud and thatch mat, which they covered with more thatch. Lastly they tied the roof down with a net of straw rope, sewing it to the rafter hoops and under the top layer of sod blocks, to keep the roof from blowing away. It was amazing to see what they built using only sod blocks, small shrubs and straw! A straw cross, tied with llama wool dyed bright red, rested at the top of the roof symbolizing the house spirit.

The single doorway had a high threshold and a low lintel to keep out some of the blowing sand. There were no windows. The door was a variety of boards and pieces of tin, or else large cactus planks stitched together with strips of pigskin. On the floor inside was a small mud stove, some sheep skins, and possibly a bundle of wool blankets or clothes.

The Chipayas' country homes were cone-shaped, made entirely of sod blocks, requiring no rafters or straw. Chipaya families spent most of their time in their country homes, near their flocks and quinoa plots, though a few people usually stayed in town.

Our House

We lived in a big storeroom until our house was built. While Ron helped build it, I took care of Debbie, cooked, washed diapers and made sure our supplies didn't walk off. The east and west sides of town were actually like two separate towns, called "*ayllus*," each with its own officials. They said that originally there had also been a north and a south ayllu but as the population dwindled, these had been incorporated into the east and west ayllus.

Since our house was on the west side of the plaza, men and women from "West-Side" built it. Some carried adobes and built the walls while others took llamas and went for straw. They were happy when Ron transported loads of adobes in the Jeep. We said we would be *Middle People* relating to both sides of town.

In two weeks our house was ready to move in, though the mud on the walls was still wet. It was about ten feet wide and thirty feet long, divided into two rooms, with a dirt floor. It had a single-pitch roof, slanting down from the fourteen-foot front wall to the seven-foot back wall. Over the eucalyptus roof poles they tied a lattice work of cane poles, added a mud and straw mat, and finished with a thick layer of straw. When Ron wasn't looking, they put a straw cross on the roof and sprinkled blood in the high corners inside the house, evidence of a sacrifice to the house spirit.

The Chipayas made the doorway between our two rooms to accommodate them, so later Ron, who was six feet three inches tall, enlarged the opening with a pick-ax and machete until he could go back and forth to the kitchen without ducking or banging his head.

Our front room/bedroom had a door and window facing east to the plaza, with a kerosene space heater on the opposite wall. An adobe bench along the south wall held the galvanized wash tub which doubled as a crib for Debbie. A trunk and our homemade bed served in lieu of chairs when visitors came.

The kitchen/dining room had a window facing the plaza, a smaller window facing north, and a back door to the west. We stapled opaque, translucent plastic to the windows. An adobe counter on the north wall of our kitchen held our camp stove, dishes, food items, etc. One end of our table top rested on a pile of adobes by the wall, and the other end on a barrel. We did have two wooden chairs. Being typical Americans, we slowly improved our living quarters. After five weeks, our house was still very damp from all the wet mud, so we stapled up a ten foot wide piece of construction plastic as a ceiling to hold down the cooking heat and dry out our living area faster. We spent most of our time in the front room/bedroom. Not much privacy that way, but when the sun went down most folks went home, so it wasn't too bad.

To begin with, our *facilities* consisted of walking out of town and finding a broken wall to squat behind. At night we used a pot and disposed of the contents in the morning. No other choices. But the air and ground were so totally dry that in a day or two everything was as dry as dust.

When Ron dug a hole for an outhouse, the neighbors asked, "What are you doing?"

They snickered when he said, "Digging a toilet hole."

He built walls with sod blocks as curious men and children asked, "Now what?"

"Building a toilet house." More snickers.

A few days later it was ready to use – hurray! It surely beat walking out to the wide open spaces beyond town. At first there was no door, but by then everyone had heard what it was and respected our privacy – except for a few curious children!

We settled into a simple lifestyle. My growing up as a missionary kid in Guatemala was a big advantage now as living simply was not a new thing, and Ron had always enjoyed being a Boy Scout. We drew water from the salty wells in town, or from the less salty river. We boiled drinking water and cooked almost everything in the pressure cooker on a kerosene camp stove, because at 12,000 feet altitude water boils at 188 degrees.

Fortunately Ron was a handy man. To keep down the moisture in our house, he put in a flagstone floor of flat rocks found a few miles away. He dug up pieces of rocks with his pickax, brought them home in the Jeep, and fit them together like a jigsaw puzzle. Strips of plastic foam around the front door served as weather stripping.

We had barely moved into our new house when Ron had to make an emergency trip to Oruro. After he left, the wind blew down the chimney of our space heater, so I had to wear extra pajamas, socks and sweaters at night to keep warm. When he got home a few days later, he moved the heater to the east wall which was higher and would give the chimney more support. Chopping through eighteen inches of adobe for the chimney raised a lot of dust, but then the heater worked great!

Chipaya Laundromat - *Not* a Quick Wash

I was grateful when a Chipaya lady named Maxine helped me wash clothes. I had to give her a special invitation each time, and this could take almost as long as the washing, but it gave me a chance to visit a little and use the few phrases I was learning.

I'd wend my way past the houses which were padlocked shut, to her house which was usually open. At the small doorway I'd say, "I've come to visit." When she said, "Come in," I'd duck my head a little and step over the high threshold. Then she'd say "Sit down," motioning to a sheepskin on the floor. Maxine's little girl, Damiana, would be playing on the dirt floor or napping under a homespun blanket. No furniture – just a three-burner mud stove on the floor with a few blackened cooking pots. No windows – just a six-inch hole half way up the wall, hoping some smoke would find its way out. Various bundles of who-knows-what completed the furnishings. Their supply of quinoa and other belongings were in an adjacent house or in their country home.

I'd ask, "What are you doing?" and she'd show me what she was spinning or cooking, explaining everything in Chipaya. After a while I'd say, "I'm washing clothes. Do you want to help?" Often she'd say, "I'll come." Then I'd say, "I'm going," and she'd say, "Go."

One day her husband, Tomas, scolded me for being so blunt, and dictated long sentences for requesting help more politely. I wish I had memorized them instead of feeling offended and defensive of my few short phrases.

Back home, I'd heat water on our camp stove on the floor. Then I'd lay Debbie in the middle of our bed, since her crib was my wash tub. We scrubbed the clothes on a small washboard then cranked them through the wringer, fastened to one end of the tub. We'd dump the soapy water out the front door, rinse the clothes and hang them on a clothesline strung from our front door post to the antenna pole. Often the first diapers were dry by the time we were ready to hang more. On cold days they'd freeze stiff. I had to wash four days a week.

One day before we dumped the soapy water Maxine asked, "May I wash Damiana's dress?" I said "Of course." When she untied Damiana's belt, I was surprised to see her *dress* was one big square cloth, pinned at the shoulders and gathered by a belt at the waist! When Maxine dressed Damiana in another large cloth, I realized Maxine's dress was just a larger rectangle, though underneath she also wore a white homespun blouse with blue sleeves.

One day a little girl wanted to help put clothes through the wringer, so I said, "Okay, but wash your hands first," as I pointed to her hands and gave her a basin of warm, soapy water. She scrubbed and scrubbed without much success until a little boy slipped her a stone to scrape off the crusted dirt. About ten minutes later when she was ready to help, the basin of water was black! After we finished washing, I put the washtub on the ground outside, then the other girls and boys crowded around to wash their hands. They even pulled out filthy hankies and scrubbed them. When they finished they spread out their hands, grinning, "They're white! They're white!"

One time a little boy announced each piece of clothing as it came through the wringer, "Socks. Shirt. Pants. Underpants," etc. When a bra came through he asked, "What's that?" I didn't stop to explain.

Mothering a Lamb

Of course Maxine always brought two-year-old Damiana, and stopped to nurse her periodically. Chipaya babies don't wear diapers, so one day we had a big wet spot on our bed where Damiana had been sitting. Another day, Maxine brought a tiny lamb as well, and after nursing Damiana she nursed the lamb. I couldn't believe my eyes. It nursed much more vigorously than Damiana did! I couldn't imagine doing that.

When I told Ron, he said, "Since the Chipayas are so poor, and their flocks are their livelihood, when mother sheep die, the women nurse the lambs till they can eat grass." Maxine wanted us to leave Debbie with her when we went to Cochabamba, but I didn't think she had enough milk for all three. We heard they did the same with piglets, but I didn't even want to see that!

Of Germs and Spirits

Diaper rash was a constant problem. Once when Ceferino was visiting Ron, he asked, "Why are you cooking the diapers?" We said, "To kill the germs that are making Debbie's skin sore." He asked, "What are germs?" Ron said, "They are like tiny animals, so tiny you can't see them, but they're there, and they can hurt you." Suddenly Ceferino's face lit up and he said, "Oh yes! Like the spirits. You can't see them, but they're there and they surely can hurt you!"

Consulting the Stars

One day I found Tomas, Maxine's husband, consulting an astrology book. When he saw me he whisked the book out of sight, looking rather disgruntled. His mother was holding a large paper with lots of little figures on it. When I said, "What a pretty paper!" she just scowled. Later, Maxine said, "My husband butchered a pig because a certain star was so bright." Apparently there was a lot going on around us that was none of our business.

Years later, Ron and a believer named Maximo translated the story about the new believers in Ephesus lighting public bonfires to burn their books about black magic and incantations (Acts 19:19). Maximo, who at that time had already been reading the Spanish New Testament, said, "We've had several of those bonfires here, too. A lot of Chipayas used to consult those books."

Quinoa with Extra Fiber!

We had heard that the Chipayas' main diet was a tiny but nutritious grain called quinoa, so we bought some and I was boiling it for lunch. A man saw me bending over our little camp stove and invited himself into our storeroom/bedroom/kitchen. He asked, "What are you doing?"

I said, "Cooking dinner."

"What are you cooking?"

"Quinoa."

"Where did you get it?"

"We bought it from someone."

"Let me see." So I lifted the lid. In disgust, he said, "It still has the husk on it. Only pigs eat it *that* way!"

"Then why didn't they tell us? How was I supposed to know?" I asked a bit aggravated.

He just shrugged his shoulders and left. Our first quinoa meal had extra fiber!

Knowing there weren't any stores in Chipaya, we had brought supplies from Oruro: flour, sugar, rice, oatmeal, KLIM (full-cream powdered milk from Holland), canned vegetables, applesauce and some fresh carrots, potatoes and onions. We also brought fresh meat which I immediately canned in ten pint jars to have one a week.

Later, when the Chipayas needed cash, they'd sell us quinoa or an animal. The only way to have meat was to buy the whole carcass skinned out. *For conscience sake* (as Apostle Paul said in 1 Cor. 10:25) we didn't ask if it had been sacrificed to the spirits. A whole two-year-old sheep only weighed eight to ten pounds since they had so little pasture. Mutton kept well in our house which was like a big walk-in cooler, so we just cut it up, hung it on nails on the kitchen rafters, and cooked a bit each day.

Quinoa, the Staff of Life

Sometimes Maxine stepped into my Laundromat and other times I stepped into her kitchen. Since quinoa was the only crop that grew around Chipaya, it was their staple. Preparing it took a long time.

One day *I tried my feet* at threshing it. First Maxine knelt by her little mud stove and lit a fire to toast the quinoa in her tin-can frying pan. I gulped when she used the same stick to stir the quinoa and to push llama dung into the fire – hopefully the flames disinfected it! Then she poured the toasted quinoa into a stone mortar outside her house and threshed it with her bare feet serving as the pestle, balancing herself with her hands on the adobe wall. She twirled back and forth, first on one foot then the other, her heavy skirt whirling this way and that. Whenever she felt a breeze, she jumped from the stone mortar into a little flat basket (to keep her feet clean), while she slowly poured handfuls of grain, so the breeze would carry off the dust-fine chaff.

I tried threshing the second batch, but my feet barely fit in the mortar and the grain was so hot I had to keep jumping up onto the stone rim of the mortar to cool my burning feet! Maxine laughed and said, "Your feet are like baby feet, but *mine* know how!" Next she winnowed the tiny grains more thoroughly by scooping up basketfuls and slowly pouring them onto a big cloth.

Since she was carrying Damiana on her back, she tied the sack of quinoa on my back. At the river, she dropped the sack in the shallow water and pushed it around with her feet till the water ran clear. She scrubbed her arms up to her elbows and her legs up to her knees in the river before we headed home where she spread the quinoa on three big cloths to dry in the sun. She gave me some to make soup for supper. It was delicious!

The next day she ground some of the quinoa into flour on her little stone grinder, like the Maya Indians use in Guatemala. Then she wet it with salty water till she could press it into hard balls, with a little sheep grease in the center. She steamed these balls in a clay pot which had wet straw in the bottom, and a straw wreath for a lid. In about half an hour they were ready to eat, dry but not bad tasting. Years later, our girls called them *sand balls* because of that extra ingredient – sand!

Maxine ground and toasted some of the quinoa again till it was medium brown. This could be eaten as a snack or like dry cereal – *very* dry cereal! We liked it with milk and sugar.

Now I could fix an all-quinoa meal: quinoa soup, quinoa bread, fluffy steamed quinoa, steamed quinoa 'balls' and quinoa cookies for dessert! It soon became our nutritious staple.

Meeting My Neighbors

One day I visited my neighbors Ilarion and Jacinta. Ilarion and I conversed in Spanish and he translated for his wife. She was doing women's work, spinning a fine, even thread of wool on a spindle. It looked easy, but when I tried, my thread was very lumpy. Ilarion was twisting two threads together and rolling them into a ball; this was men's work. It takes many balls to weave each piece of clothing.

They asked, "How many godparents does your baby have?"

I answered, "None. How many do Chipaya children have?"

"At least one, but two if they are baptized." Then he asked, "How many are in your family?"

I said, "Seven."

"Seven! That's a lot! Did any die?"

"No."

"Chipayas don't have so many children, and a lot of babies die here."

I asked, "Do you have any children?"

"No."

"How long have you been married?"

"Several years."

We had heard the birthrate on the *altiplano* was one of the lowest in the world. Several young women had already said, "Regalame tu wawita." (Please give me your baby!)

We talked about spinning, weaving, preparing quinoa, caring for animals, etc.

Ilarion said, "Pigs eat almost anything but we never give them flour or bread because that gives them trichinosis. But few people have trichinosis because most pig owners are careful."

When women, children and even men asked why I didn't nurse my baby, I'd say, "I don't have very much milk." One day a lady puzzled over it for a while then said, "My baby is big but I still have plenty of milk, see..." and she pulled her blouse open and squirted in the air a few times! Then, with an embarrassed laugh, she ducked her head and scooted away. If I had been able to nurse Debbie, I could have identified more easily with the women.

Yunguyo's Arrows

One windy afternoon there was a strong electrical storm, which would have burned out our radio if Ron hadn't disconnected it from the antenna. Sparks jumped three-quarters of an inch from the antenna wire which hung on a big nail in the wall. There was a continual buzzing and popping for over fifteen minutes.

Just then Ilarion happened by. I was showing him the sparks at the end of the antenna when suddenly I got a shock and jumped! He asked, "What happened?"

I said, "The electricity grabbed me. Do you know about electricity?"

"No."

I said, "It comes from the lightning. Touch the metal end of the antenna and you'll see." He touched it. Nothing. He touched it again. Nothing.

I said, "Lick your finger then touch it."

He did, then bang! This time he really jumped. His eyes grew big as saucers, and he was out of there!

Later Ceferino told us, "The Chipayas believe that the apostles, Peter, Philip, James and Yunguyo [You didn't know Yunguyo was an apostle? Well, neither did we!], gallop through the heavens on horses, causing thunder and shooting flaming arrows at the demons. When lightning strikes a person it means the devil or demons are hiding in him. When it strikes a house, it is punishing the owners, and the house is taboo." No wonder Ilarion was so scared!

Ceferino added, "Several houses are struck by lightning and burned every year. Last year a fellow was struck and killed while riding his bike across the *altiplano*." With our high radio antenna pole we were a likely object. We decided to get a lightning rod the next time we were in Oruro.

Is the Doctor In?

Ron was the only doctor in Chipaya. Knowing that would be the case, we had brought basic medicines – pain pills, sulfa pills and antibiotics. His only medical training was a health course during training camp in Mexico before coming to Bolivia, but we had a *Merck Manual* and we could consult by radio with nurses at our mission center in the jungle. (Since most language groups lived in the lowlands, our mission headquarters were by a small lake in the jungle.)

The most common complaints were stomach problems and coughs. As our medicines cured people, parents brought babies with diarrhea. Depending on the baby's size, we crushed part of a sulfa pill in a spoon, added a bit of sugar and water, and fed it to the baby, then had the mother nurse it to make sure it swallowed the medicine. Then we'd give the parents enough medicine and sugar for a couple days, and have them repeat the instructions. One man asked, "Can't we just mash the pill and rub it on her stomach?" Ron said, "This kind of medicine doesn't work that way." When he gave liquid medicine to a lady for her baby, he said, "Shake it well first." She innocently asked, "Shake the baby?"

When they saw me powdering Debbie, they asked. "Is that DDT?"

The Chipayas believed that puncturing the skin allowed *Heat* and *Cold* (which had no relation to temperature) to enter the body and cause sickness, so Ron seldom gave shots.

Ron also treated eyes, ears, fevers and chills. One day a lady came because her ear was painful and draining. It smelled so bad he had to hold his breath while he bent over to clean it. Besides the foul odor from the infection, her whole head stunk of fermented urine. Some old folks still used this homemade ammonia to wash their hair, saying it killed the lice and left the hair nice and shiny. In this case it almost wiped out the doctor!

Another time a man cut his hand with a hoe but he didn't come for medicine until the cut was oozing, and a terrible infection had spread up his arm. Daily applications of Watkin's Carbo-Petro black salve slowly drew out the infection and eventually healed his arm and hand.

A few weeks after we arrived, Ron was called to see a very weak man who was wheezing with chest pains – apparently from pneumonia. Tetracycline capsules worked wonders in a few days. Then a man came saying his wife was coughing up blood. Tetracycline also helped her recover in a few days as strong antibiotics did wonders for people who hadn't had them before.

Once Ron even treated a sick chicken. He mashed up a piece of a sulfa pill, mixed it with a bit of water, and poured it down the chicken's throat. The owner was amazed when it recovered!

One day people said, "The mayor of East-Side had an *attack* last night. He acted like he was drunk, took off all his clothes, and did other strange things – but in the morning he was normal again. Rituals and blood sacrifices cured him." Their description sounded like demon possession.

The Second Opinion

Medical work, however, was a bit risky because people came to us for a second opinion after consulting the shaman. We always prayed for wisdom and God's healing. If they recovered, the shaman probably took the credit and if they got worse, they could blame us.

The shamans' diagnosis for sickness or natural calamities was usually a disgruntled spirit which was demanding an animal sacrifice or an ancestor or enemy whose curse often required several animal sacrifices to break the spell.

Occasionally, there was a different diagnosis. When a baby's stomach was swollen from constipation, the diviners said, "It's because he slept outside and the heat of the sun entered him and now his heart is swollen and he's almost dead." After making a sacrifice, the father came to Ron who gave him liquid vitamins.

One day the mayor said, "Day before yesterday my three-year-old son fell head first into a shallow well. He was almost dead and since then he hasn't eaten well, and always wants to stay close to his mother. His *animo* (spirit) was so frightened it must have fled. We need a powerful shaman to bring his spirit back."

The Chipayas also had a few *home remedies* of their own. For fever, they made tea from horrible-tasting *lampaya* leaves, and for colds and chills they made tea from the root of a spiny plant. Tea made by boiling bats was considered a powerful cure for seizures. For sores and cuts they tried to find a whole little lizard to tie over the wound for a day or two.

One day a man had an *attack* and fell head first off the house he was helping to roof, landing on the side of his head and on his shoulder, breaking his collar bone. While children ran to catch lizards to patch on his shoulder, Ron gave him pain killers and put on a modified figure-eight bandage for support.

Joey

A month after we arrived we were just finishing breakfast when a man asked for medicine for his boy's *swelling.* Ron found the boy lying on the ground near a ball. The swelling was about three inches above the ankle, probably a broken leg. They carried him home on a bicycle while Ron went to get bandages, wood for a splint, and aspirins. When he returned they said, "Yes, it's broken. We can hear the bones rubbing against each other," as they twisted the boy's foot back and forth. Poor little Joey was crying and trembling from head to toe with pain. Ron gave him aspirins, made a splint, and told them not to move him. His father asked, "Do you have medicine to heal bones?" Ron said "No, but I'll check by radio tomorrow." We thought calcium might help, but we didn't have any. Ron repeated, "Don't move him!" and emphasized it again that evening.

When he went to check on Joey in the morning, they had taken off the splint and plastered his leg with a concoction of urine and cornmeal, then tied the splint back on. They had moved him again. Of course his leg was more swollen. They were drunk, since there was a fiesta going on. What else could we do? The next time Ron went to check on him, the house was locked up. They had taken him to their country home.

Mr. Fix-It

The Chipayas either walked or rode bicycles. Often men came on Sundays to buy a bit of machine oil or for Ron to fix a flat tire or a bent rim. They were happy when he brought bicycle parts from Oruro. Some weekends Ron operated a mini bicycle repair shop in front of our house, where they could all use our tools. They didn't want a store in town because they didn't want anyone to make a profit off of them so they each bicycled to Escara or other towns for sugar, flour, or whatever else they wanted.

Just being friendly and helpful took a lot of time. When Ron fixed a radio that had a loose wire, the word spread and Chipayas brought radios, flashlights, bulbs, and padlocks to be fixed! He always said, "I'll try," and often succeeded.

We also tried to help them settle their land disputes by having our mission representative in La Paz set up a court hearing for them in the city. Then the mayor brought two long hand-written pages of documents for Ron to type, asserting the land was theirs. Some of the documents dated from 1722 – when George Washington was a boy! It took Ron several hours to decipher and type them on our manual typewriter.

Our village living also provided many do-it-yourself experiences. Our spatula was too hard and stiff for turning pancakes, so Ron made a new one. He cut the top and bottom off a tin can then cut down the side of the can and flattened it, rounding the corners. It worked beautifully. Half of a flattened #10 KLIM can made a cookie sheet just the right size for our little oven. My bottle brush was strips of plastic sponge with wire twisted around them, and wire for the handle. Adobes served well as a wash basin stand, legs for a bed frame, table legs, and also served to elevate our oven so the pressure camp stove fit under it for baking.

Unscrambling the ABC's

Ron wrote down every word he heard, using the International Phonetic Alphabet we had learned at the Summer Institute of Linguistics (SIL) in Oklahoma. Chipaya vowels were usually *a, i* or *u* with an occasional *e* or *o*. When they used Spanish words, they changed *o* to *u* and *e* to *i*. They didn't use *b, d, f* or *g* sounds in their language, so when they borrowed Spanish words the *b* became *p*, *d* became *t*, and *g* became *k*. Debbie Sue became *Tepi Sulya*, and *adobe* became *atupi*.

For a week, Ceferino worked on the language with Ron. We were so thankful for his help. Ron wrote each word on an index card with its Spanish and English equivalent, charting all the words with similar sounds.

As a teenager, Ceferino had clashed with his step-father, so he had gone to work in Chile as Chipaya men often did. Returning to Chipaya years later, he was on the fringe of society and friendly toward outsiders, including the two translators who had preceded us. While attending a Christian meeting with the second couple in an Aymara town, Ceferino had decided to worship God instead of the capricious spirits. When he wouldn't take part in the fiestas nor sacrifice to the spirits, he was ostracized by the other Chipayas.

Working with Ceferino, Ron discovered two c sounds (we wrote *c* and *k*), three *s* sounds (*s, z* and *zh*), and two *ch* sounds, one of which was written with a tilde over the c. What sounded like *acha* could mean head or llama dung. You say your llama dung hurts? There was also a *ts* sound. He discovered that seven consonants (*p, t, c, k, ch, ch [with a tilde],ts*) could be pronounced softly, with a puff of air or with a click. The alphabet was getting longer!

Chipaya also had voiceless vowels, like whispered vowels, which had to be written differently– but how? That was the question.

One good week of language help was followed by a lean week, as Ceferino went to Oruro. Then Ron concentrated on memorizing vocabulary and looking for others to help us learn their language.

We were delighted when a bright, friendly fellow named Anselmo offered to help. Ron concentrated on the *s* sounds that were very similar, but gave words different meanings. By combining different *s* and *k* sounds, what sounded like *skara* to our ears, could mean any of five things: a man's hat, a hawk, a frog, a fork in a road, or left-handed. By the way, that's a nice frog you're wearing today. And did you see how far that hat jumped?

A couple days later Ron went looking for Anselmo, who had said he would come again. This time he gave wrong words, and wouldn't give the meaning of others. It was a frustrating morning. Afterward, when they were just relaxing in the sun, Anselmo asked, "Why are you here, anyway?" Apparently over the weekend he had been influenced against us, and never helped again.

A few days later, the man who had almost died from pneumonia came to visit. Ron talked in Chipaya as much as he could. When the man used a couple words Ron hadn't heard before, Ron reached for paper and a pencil and wrote them down. The man gave a knowing smile, and asked, "How much are you paid for each word?"

"I'm not paid anything. We just want to learn your language so we can make books for you, and translate God's Book."

The man's sneer said, "Yeah. Right! If you aren't making a profit off our language, why do you want to live here?"

It was disheartening to save a man's life and have him turn against you. We wondered if Ceferino would be the only one to help us learn the language. Thank goodness for Ceferino!

A week or two later a friendly fellow named Eulogio said he'd teach us, and worked with Ron a couple days. He wasn't the brightest, but he was helpful. He called the back *s* a *z*. That sounded like a good idea, so Ron wrote it that way. The sounds were so similar we could hardly tell them apart. Some words I didn't dare use for fear of mispronouncing them so they meant something else! Ron hoped to have the Chipaya alphabet figured out so we could have it approved by a linguistic consultant when we went to Cochabamba in a few weeks.

Worship in Three Languages

One Sunday Ron and Ceferino drove beyond the river to meet with an Aymara family. They read from the Spanish Bible, discussed the passage and sang in Aymara, and prayed in Chipaya. Though they were very poor, the family insisted on giving Ron a few potatoes and eggs – which he carried home *very* carefully!

Ceferino often came on Sundays to sing and read the Spanish Bible and he remembered tunes well. Sometimes others stopped by when they heard us singing. They had never sung before, because their fiesta tunes didn't have words.

One week Ron was sitting in the sun chatting with three or four men. As Ceferino approached, a fellow said, "He's coming to sing." Then a young fellow named Florencio rode up on his bike and said, "Let's all sing!" So they all came inside and sang from Ceferino's Aymara-Spanish hymnbook for about an hour. From then on, we sang hymns on Sundays with whoever happened to show up.

Though the Chipayas ostracized Ceferino for not taking part in the fiestas and rituals, at the same time they seemed to respect him.

New Friends

Several mornings a week we checked in by two-way radio with our mission headquarters, for news from co-workers in the city and at the jungle center. Before long an electrical storm shorted out our radio. The agreement was that if we were off the air for five consecutive days, our director would send someone to check on us. There was no choice but for Ron to make another emergency trip to Oruro for a new radio.

After Ron left, it was quiet around town – until a Canadian and a Bolivian priest arrived. Debbie and I joined the crowd to greet them and I said, "Hello. Welcome." They said, "Hello. How long have you been here?" I said, "About a month. Could I fix you some supper?" "No thanks. We have canned goods." Chipaya was too small a town for non-friends, so a couple days later I took them some fresh sweet rolls and asked for help using a big stapler. I guess the sweet rolls melted the ice for the Canadian priest, Padre Amado, because before long he said, "If you run low on flour, sugar or kerosene, just let us know. We have some in our storeroom." Hurray! We had a new friend!

They left that afternoon, saying, "We'll be back in a few days."

The "Madrecita"

Mid-October, Padre Amado returned with Juanina, a stocky little French Canadian nun whom the Chipayas called *la Madrecita* – Little Mother. We joined the crowd and Ron helped unload their green station wagon. Madrecita Juanina was very cool. She had clashed with the previous translators, so everyone was waiting to see sparks fly. They said she usually came with a partner but this time she was alone, having just returned from Canada.

The next morning Padre Amado returned to the Catholic mission station in Huachacalla. We saw the Madrecita walking around town a number of times, but she never came by our house. Each school morning she served the students CARE oatmeal which the Chipayas cooked in a half barrel over an open llama-dung fire. The smoke must have flavored the oatmeal, but the children didn't seem to mind. Any warm food tasted good on a cold morning.

About then, Debbie caught a cold, which she couldn't shake. After taking antibiotics for a couple weeks, she got a rash. Hearing that Juanina was a nurse, I asked her to please come see Debbie.

She seemed pleased that we asked her for help. When she saw our sick baby lying in her wash-tub crib, she said, "Pobrecita! (Poor little thing!) Maybe the rash is a reaction to the medicine," so we stopped giving it. A couple days later Debbie's rash was clearing but her eye was swollen. Fortunately we had eye ointment. A few days later two teeth broke though and her eye cleared up, but her cold and cough continued. Occasionally now Juanina asked how Debbie was doing. We prayed she wouldn't get pneumonia. She was only five months old.

A week later, two boys pounded on our door saying, "The Madrecita is sick! She wants you to come." Ron found her lying in bed with a temperature of 104 degrees and pulse of 140. She said, "I'm sorry to bother you, but I'm afraid I'm going to die!" Ron said, "It's no bother. We're glad you called," and he gave her Tetracycline.

When he told me how sick she was, I left Debbie with him, took a sleeping bag and insisted on staying with her overnight. Her room was very simple: just a few blankets on an adobe bed, a chair and a little table, and a crucifix on the wall. Poor thing! She was so sick and so scared! We loaned her an air mattress and a foam pillow then prayed together for a good night's sleep and for healing. I told her to call me if she woke up and needed anything. Soon she fell asleep. I had a hard time getting comfortable on my adobe bed, but finally fell asleep as well. To everyone's relief, she seemed better the next day.

In the morning when I opened the door to serve breakfast to the school children, their eyes almost popped out! They kept looking at me and whispering to each other as I filled their bowls. It was fun to watch their expressions. They couldn't imagine what I was doing in the Madrecita's house!

She had called Padre Amado by radio the day before, so we were happy for him to take over when he arrived that morning.

News of the sick Madrecita and my sleeping in her house spread like wildfire. My friend Maxine dropped by and asked, "Did she have her baby?" I said, "No. She is just very sick. She's not going to have a baby." But Maxine insisted, "She was fat last year and didn't have a baby, so surely she is going to have one *this* year!" I said, "No. She's just a little bit fat," but I'm sure she didn't believe me because there are no fat Chipayas – life is too hard and quinoa has no starch!

That evening Padre Amado knocked urgently on our door saying, "She's worse! Please come!" so Ron hurried over. This time she wanted Penicillin, so Ron gave her a shot, his first since training camp in southern Mexico. That night her fever broke and she was better in the morning. Whereas she had been very aloof, now we were friends forever.

Race for Life

As the Madrecita got better, Debbie got worse and we had no other medicine. We decided to take her to Oruro, leaving early Saturday morning with the Jeep loaded to capacity. In Escara we stopped to tell the school director we'd be back in a month or so. When he saw we were going to Oruro he said, "I need to go, too! Please take me." Ron said, "Sorry. We don't have room, and we need to get our baby to the doctor quickly." He said, "Just leave some of your baggage, and I'll have it sent on the very next truck." So we quickly unloaded everything accept our language materials and a few clothes to make room for him and his baggage.

This was Ron's eighth time over these roads in three months, but only my second. We didn't stop for anything – rivers, sand or ruts. I held a limp baby in my arms but couldn't get her to drink. We prayed all the way, "Dear Lord Jesus, please help us get her to a doctor in time. Please don't let us lose her. Please, Father..." About noon I started getting a sick headache which worsened by the hour. Although we raced against time, the trip still took nine hours.

When we reached our missionary friends' house, I collapsed under a pile of blankets with chills and a splitting headache while Ron took Debbie to the doctor. His verdict: "Severe bronchitis, almost pneumonia. Give her this medicine every four hours." Ron said, "We plan to fly to Cochabamba on Monday." He said, "No way. She's much too sick for a plane flight."

None of us slept much that night. Debbie threw up most of the medicine we gave her, but apparently got enough to be much better the next day. We were *so* thankful. Sunday afternoon the doctor even gave permission for her to fly, so by Monday noon we reached Cochabamba, exhausted and bedraggled but very thankful for a twenty-five minute flight instead of an eight or nine-hour train trip. It was wonderful to be back in the mission house with our friends and colleagues.

We'd been in Chipaya less than three months but it felt like a lifetime.

THE FIRST RAINY SEASON

We spent a couple weeks in Cochabamba while Debbie recovered and Ron worked on the Chipaya alphabet. A linguistic consultant gave tentative approval for our alphabet, based on the 3000 words Ron had collected.

When we returned to Chipaya, the Madrecita was gone. Padre Amado had moved her back to their mission center so she wouldn't be stranded on the wrong side of the Lauca River all rainy season. Now the Chipayas were more at ease coming to our house and showing an interest in the Gospel. They liked the large Bible pictures hanging on our wall, with Spanish verses printed under them. One day when Tomas read the verses, Ron showed him where they were found in the Bible. As he expressed interest, Ron explained a bit more. Tomas gave a rough translation of a couple verses but admitted, "I don't really understand this Spanish very well."

Language work

Now Ron was trying to figure out how Chipaya words and sentences fit together. Hearing everybody talk so fast, I asked Ron, "How do you know where to start?" He said, "It's what they taught us at SIL, remember?" I remembered studying hard, but it hadn't stuck with me. Fortunately I had married a "straight A" linguist! We welcomed Ceferino when he came to help dissect the long verbs, explaining the sets of suffixes which told who, when, why and how someone did something.

Meanwhile I tried memorizing phrases while washing clothes or caring for Debbie, but it didn't work. In my spare moments, however, I learned a few phrases, started planning a Bible story book, and sketched objects around town to illustrate an alphabet book. We needed two or three picture words for each letter, a total of over a hundred illustrations. We wanted to print a booklet soon so the Chipayas could see their language in writing, especially since the Aymaras who surrounded them said, "Your language *can't* be written because it isn't a *real* language like Aymara and Spanish."

Our First Christmas

The night before we returned to Chipaya, our missionary friend in Oruro had asked, "Do you have any Christmas decorations?" I said, "Oops! We haven't even thought about Christmas!" After all, it wasn't even Thanksgiving yet. In the morning she gave us a ten-inch tree made of green construction paper, decorated with tiny paper balls, Japanese lanterns, stars, and a red and white crepe paper rope. She had stayed up late to provide a little Christmas atmosphere for our new home!

We had an afghan which Ron's Mom had made, crocheting around rectangular blocks of dark material. For Christmas we draped the afghan over our trunk to look like a brick fireplace, and colored a paper to simulate a fire. Then we stood the little paper tree and a homemade Christmas card on the *mantel* and hung one of my stockings on the *fireplace* with Debbie's favorite toys in it, since we had forgotten to buy her any presents. Most of the Christmas music on the radio was "Jingle Bells," but we read the Christmas story from the Bible and sang all the carols we knew.

During Christmas week, after we washed clothes, Maxine invited me for a food gift in the evening. I accepted, not realizing I would witness a very different kind of Christmas – as seen through the eyes of a boy named Aurelio...

* * * * *

Chipaya Christmas

When you think of Christmas, what comes to mind? Gifts? Trees? Lights? Maybe Sunday school programs and Christ whose birthday we celebrate?

This story is about a completely different Christmas – that of a young boy named Aurelio. He is a real boy who lives in the little village of Chipaya high on a barren plateau in Bolivia. Aurelio had never heard about Christmas.

The sunshine was streaming in through the doorway when Aurelio woke up. He sat up on his sheepskin bed and rubbed his eyes. He didn't need to get dressed. The clothes he slept in were the same ones he wore all day – the only ones he had.

Over by the mud stove on the floor of his round hut, sat a little basket of dry quinoa meal. Aurelio scooped a few handfuls and popped them into his mouth. Happily, he suddenly remembered that today was a special fiesta day. That meant lots of meat, soup and all the moist, fluffy quinoa he could eat that night.

There was no Christmas tree in Aurelio's house, because there are no trees at all in Chipaya. In the foreigners' house he had seen a branch of an evergreen shrub planted in a pail of sand, with shiny balls and tinsel on it. He liked to look at it, but wasn't sure why it was there. His little round house, like all other Chipaya houses, just had sooty mud walls, a straw roof and a dirt floor covered by a few dusty animal skins.

Aurelio didn't know that in some places children received gifts at Christmas. He didn't even have any toys, except for a rag ball. And a little car made from a scrap of wood with four tin-can lids nailed on for wheels. Of course, he didn't need many toys because he had fun playing with the animals. The piglets were especially fun to play with because they squealed so loud when he held up their front feet and made them dance on their hind feet. But his favorite pet was a little white lamb, which he called *Chunka* because it was so woolly and soft.

As he stepped out over the high doorstep, Aurelio could see this was a special day. People were hurrying everywhere, and everyone seemed busy and happy. Those who had new fiesta clothes were wearing them today. Here and there a woman was sitting on the ground while two other ladies busily braided her hair into a hundred long, tiny braids. The men were cleaning sheep or llama skins or cutting up the meat, while the women poked llama-dung fuel into the popping open fires. Five-gallon square alcohol cans or cut-off barrels served as cooking pots for boiling the meat and quinoa soup. It made Aurelio's mouth water just to think of the evening meal.

Since no one needed his help, Aurelio looked for his brother Felix and the other big boys and spent most of the day following them around.

When the sun began to dip down in the west, families started to gather at their houses. Aurelio knew the feast-day rituals would start soon. He and all his family believed that performing these rituals would make their flocks of sheep and llamas multiply in the coming year.

Aurelio ran home. His brother Felix already had a big cloth of fluffy quinoa tied on his back and carried a white banner on a cane pole. His mother handed Aurelio a basket of clay bowls and a rusty tin can with flowers from the mountains. Though wilted, the flowers were special, because flowers don't grow in Chipaya. His uncle had biked several hours to find these. Then his mother and aunt picked up the five-gallon can of soup and led the way out of town.

As they headed toward the family corrals out on the sandy plateau, they could see other families gathering by their corrals. When they reached theirs, several women were already there, and Aurelio's uncle was tending a wispy fire.

Members of his family gathered from different directions, driving small flocks of sheep. In the distance Aurelio saw his grandfather and ran to meet him so he could carry Chunka, his little lamb. He held it close, resting his chin on its woolly head. The men herded the sheep into the round corral until it almost overflowed. As they strung a rope across the narrow entrance, Aurelio squeezed little Chunka in close to its mother. Then his father, carrying a baby llama, led the mother llama and a small herd into the square corral.

Now that all was ready, Aurelio's Uncle Tomas poked a sacred stick in the hard ground, spread some new ropes and special woolly bags in front of it, then knelt down and started praying to the spirits. When he finished praying, Tomas and several adults formed a circle around a lamb on the ground, sprinkling it with alcohol and coca leaves.

Aurelio had seen so many sacrifices that he hardly noticed when his father bent over the lamb with a little knife, or when his uncle caught some blood in a small tin bowl and dashed over to throw it on the live llamas and sheep. He watched them sprinkle blood in the four cardinal directions to win the favor of all the saints and demons and ancestors and nature spirits. Aurelio hoped the spirits had noticed and would be pleased.

Next they placed clay bowls of food and burning incense on the corral walls. Then Tomas took more burning incense and ducked under the ropes into the llama corral to kneel and pray to the animals. After praying by the llamas he reached into the sheep corral and fished out another lamb. With a start, Aurelio saw it was his own little Chunka that Tomas had caught.

"Oh, no, not that one! That's mine!" he cried, but his uncle just laughed and brushed him aside.

As before, the family formed a circle around the lamb and sprinkled it with coca leaves and alcohol. But Aurelio couldn't bear to watch any more. He ran around to the back of the corrals and buried his face in his tunic. He couldn't let anyone see him cry.

Before long he heard everyone laughing and talking. He knew they were serving the soup and pouring the fluffy quinoa on big cloths so everyone could help themselves. All day Aurelio had been waiting for this feast, but now he couldn't stand the thought of food. After a while, though, his hunger got the best of him. He wiped his eyes and slipped around to eat a few handfuls of quinoa and drink a little lukewarm soup.

Later that Christmas night as Aurelio curled up on his sheepskin bed, the tears came again. Why did it have to be *his* lamb that was sacrificed? Why?

He didn't know that long ago on the first Christmas night Jesus came into the world to be the Lamb of God. He didn't know that Jesus Himself had died so that Aurelio and the other Chipayas could simply believe in Him, receive Him as their Savior, and never need to sacrifice any more of their lambs.

He didn't know – so finally he just cried himself to sleep.

This was Aurelio's Christmas. This was Christmas in Chipaya. [2]

Going Native

In February Ron was able to buy an *ira*, a man's striped tunic, plus a knitted cap with ear flaps and a felt hat. Later I bought a lady's dress and belt. I sewed an inner blouse from a flour sack adding sleeves from a scrap of blue cloth, because I couldn't stand scratchy wool next to my skin. The Chipayas enjoyed seeing us wear their clothes every day. They liked it even better when Jacinta and Modesta (Ceferino's sister) braided my hair as I sat on the ground with one lady braiding each side. It was a long, painful process. They pulled so hard I thought they'd pull the braids right off my head. Since my hair was thinner and shorter than theirs, they added dark yarn into each braid. Even so, I only ended up with seventy-seven braids, instead of one hundred twenty like many of them had. The advantage of this hair style was that it didn't tangle in the wind, or need combing for the next few weeks!

They liked to see Debbie wear a little black knitted cap like their baby girls wore and liked to feel her soft, blond hair. One lady asked, "Is it always this color or do you paint it?" Boys wore white knitted caps with bright designs. When Debbie was about nine months old, she'd often hold out one of her toys and say "*Tsss, tsss.*" They were sure she was saying "*Tish, tish*" (Here it is) and marveled at her speaking Chipaya before she was a year old!

Fiestas

Flutes squeaked and drums beat their rhythm all night long, signaling the start of another fiesta. *Fiesta* sounds like a happy party but in Chipaya it meant animal sacrifices to appease whatever spirit they were honoring, and drinking and dancing for at least a night and a day. By then men and women were in a drunken stupor, and couldn't always find their way home. Babies carried on their mothers' backs often got pneumonia from exposure to the bitter cold. Infant mortality was high.

Older folks admitted, "In the past, the two sides of town used to have big fights when they were drunk during fiestas, even killing each other. Some old folks still want to carry the grudges, but younger men don't." Now they mostly ignored each other.

The Chipayas' lives revolved around trying to appease the spirits with animal sacrifices. Nature spirits were called *Virgenes* and demons called *Mallcus*. They sacrificed to the river spirit before diverting the water, to ground spirits before planting, to animal spirits so they would reproduce, and to house spirits for protection from lightning or other ills. With each sacrifice, they poured blood on the ground to the main spirit being appeased, then sprinkled blood in the four cardinal directions to include all the spirits so they wouldn't be offended and retaliate. In times of sickness or other misfortunes, the shamans divined which spirit was demanding a sacrifice. Evil spirits were the only ones to worry about because they could harm you.

Each town official was caretaker of a staff called a *Father King*, which they worshiped as a representation of the spirit of their side of town. Mayors had red staffs and other officials had yellow ones. The staffs actually consisted of a male and a more slender female staff bound together. The officials carried them to all town meetings and important functions.

When a bell was taken from the Chipaya church tower to a new church in the Chipaya settlement of Ayparavi, three families got sick. The shamans divined the bell was unhappy there, so they appeased it with sacrifices and returned it to its original location.

On New Year's Day all the authorities were sworn in with sacrifices, dancing and drinking. On January 20, the West-Side made sacrifices to the Lauca River demon to make sure it provided the water they needed. That same day the East-Side had rituals to stop the worms which were eating their quinoa plants.

Early harvest festivals coincided with Carnival, or Mardi Gras, usually in February, when they carried samples of their first fruits on their backs. At this time they appointed Ceferino to keep the animals away from the quinoa crops, knowing he wouldn't be drunk like everyone else. During this fiesta the band marched back and forth between East-Side and West-Side, two couples danced along in front, holding hands, sort of trotting, and turning circles. A man burning incense trailed along behind. In the afternoon they carried a two-foot gilded image of *La Virgen* from the god-house to the church tower and back again. On the last round, a man wearing a monkey mask brought up the rear.

We asked Ceferino if the image belonged to the priests. He said, "No. These Oblate priests don't approve of images, nor say mass to the saints. Some people even call them 'Evangelical Priests.'"

Sacred objects abounded and all Chipaya houses had blood spots on the outside wall near the door and on the inside wall opposite the door. Even Ceferino's house had a straw cross on the roof and a small dried up carcass hanging on the wall. Ron wondered if it was a flamingo or a very small sheep or llama fetus.

One advantage of all their rituals was that they understood the need and the price of a sacrifice, and had the vocabulary to talk about it. Their lifestyle as shepherds and farmers was also close to that of the Jews in Jesus' time. They would probably understand some Scriptures better than we did.

Ron was low on gas for the Jeep just then, so during Carnival he drove to Escara to try to buy some. However, he found a fiesta in full swing there, too, with the school director providing food and drinks for about a hundred people. Men and women had rented colorful, elaborate, expensive costumes in Oruro, depicting demons, an angel, a bear, and a king and queen. Ron saw officials he had met in other towns on his first trip to Chipaya, but all were drunk, and offering him drinks. It was hard to keep refusing graciously. He decided it was best to just stay away in the future.

The God-Houses

One afternoon we heard chanting behind our house and saw ten or fifteen men, women and children sitting or kneeling by the large altar in front of the god-house, drinking and pouring something on the altar.

When a little boy happened by our house we asked him, "What are they doing?"

He said, "It's the fiesta of Saint Michael."

We asked, "Are they worshiping Saint Michael?"

No answer.

"Does every family have a special saint?"

"No."

"Is St. Michael this family's saint?"

The boy gave us a curious look, mumbled something, and walked away.

We learned that designated families killed a sheep and splashed its blood on the altar outside, and on another altar inside each of the god-houses. Later they ate the ritual meal by the altar. That night we heard frenzied music and saw a bonfire on East-Side. The next day an Aymara teacher said, "They danced around the bonfire like Redskins waving tomahawks!"

One day, when the town was deserted, Ron and I peeked between the double doors of the god-house then went inside. Blood was splattered on the adobe altar, walls and on numerous little idols in boxes and shrines. An ancient pewter-like chandelier hung from the ceiling. In the back stood two straight chairs of carved wood and engraved leather, plus an antique organ with hand bellows.

One day a mission doctor visiting Chipaya went to check out the god-house. Ron had asked him not to go in because his visit could be interpreted wrongly, but that day the entire population had gone out to the airstrip to welcome an approaching plane, and the village was empty. Seeing his chance, he went through the door and found himself in a space measuring some eight by ten feet. In the middle stood a rectangular pedestal made of clay, with red-brown stains – no doubt blood. It was about five feet tall, and on it rested a glass case. Within the case was a man mounted on a horse, equipped with a sword. On his head was a steel helmet with a swept-up point front and back, such as worn by Spanish soldiers in the sixteenth century. A conquistador, evidently.

The visitor was greatly intrigued by this discovery, but before he could investigate further he was overtaken by an eerie sense of oppression. Realizing this was an evil presence, he instinctively invoked the name of Jesus. He left the place quickly and stepped outside. There, in the open air, the oppression lifted.

Today Is ...

Each day of the week had a special significance for the Chipayas:

On Monday heaven opened for souls of the dead to visit the earth and hear people's prayers.

Tuesday and Friday were bad days, when hungry demons and ancestors came looking for sacrifices. If they didn't find any, they could eat a person's spirit, and he or she would die unless the shaman ordered the correct sacrifice. These were the nights when ancestor spirits appeared as balls of light roaming around the graves, then whoever saw this glowing *Kaka* trembled in fear, wondering which family member would die.

Wednesday and Thursday were good days.

Saturday belonged to the goddess of the earth.

Sunday belonged to God and the saints.

"Are these demons?"

As we considered printing Bible stories in Chipaya, we wondered what kind of illustrations the Chipayas would understand best. Some Bible pictures were so detailed we thought they would be confusing. Would black and white line drawings be best?

One day Ron showed Hercules the Gospel of Mark in simple Spanish, which had line drawings of people but didn't show their facial features. Hercules asked, "Are these demons?"

Ron said, "No, why?"

Hercules said, "Before the sun came, the demons had bodies. Now they are only spirits and don't have faces."

Ron said, "These are just simple drawings of people," and went on to explain the pictures.

Though we still had questions about illustrations, we knew that even simple line drawings would need to show facial features.

Foreign Magic

Ron and I came from a foreign world with tools which seemed like magic to the Chipayas.

The airplane was most impressive.

Our director said, "You should make an airstrip so we could fly you out in case of emergency. And besides, I'd like to visit you in January!" Wycliffe's technical arm, JAARS (short for Jungle Aviation And Radio Service), had been created because many Wycliffe translators lived in isolated jungle areas where there weren't any roads.

The Chipayas were willing to help smooth an airstrip if we paid them. It wasn't a very big job because there weren't any trees or shrubs to clear, only low spots to fill in or smooth over. But Ron wondered how to mark the landing strip so it could be seen from the air. When he and a couple helpers went in search of the white clay they used to mark their doorways, they got stuck in the river for three and a half hours. In the end, they piled up sod blocks like a row of pillars on either side of the runway, hoping the pilot could see them from the air.

On January 2 Ron told the Chipayas, "Our mission plane is coming." Men crowded around him as he guided the pilot by radio. Ron said, "They passed Oruro now." And a while later, "Now they see the Escara mountain and the Lauca River." The men said, "Yeah, yeah," but no one moved. Then Ron said, "Go outside and see if you can hear it." Suddenly the plane buzzed low over the town! The men ducked instinctively, then jumped on their bicycles and took off for the airstrip. They had never seen a plane up close before and they were amazed that such a heavy object could fly! Ron tried to explain how big the jets were, but they couldn't fathom that.

Word spread like wildfire that officials were flying in the next day. Somehow that flight got mixed up in their minds with the supposed war with Chile over diverting the Lauca River and they said, "It's coming to rob and kill us!" We said, "No, no. It's just a friendly visit!"

It was a red-letter day when the Minister of Rural Affairs and the Chief of Primary Education flew in from La Paz. Mayors from several towns and the football team from Escara came to greet them. When the authorities saw that the classrooms had only a few benches and two blackboards, they promised a lot of school supplies. And because the beginning students spoke only Chipaya and the teachers didn't know Chipaya, the officials invited four young men to study in a school near La Paz, to become school teachers. It sounded very promising and four young men agreed to go, but as soon as the government officials left, they all backed out. It took Ron two days to finally recruit four others. The older men said, "If anyone wants to go, okay. If not, so what? It's just for their own personal good, so why should we encourage them?"

Unfortunately, the four young men returned a few months later. They said they were served the last burnt scrapings in the food line, they weren't placed in the right classes, and all the other students called them *Stupid Indians* and made fun of them. No wonder they left.

The Radio was another magic tool which seemed to know everything. A couple days after the plane came, two young fellows told Ron, "A poor widow has been robbed. Some thieves stole all her sheep cheeses. She needs your help." Ron asked, "What can I do to help?" They said, "Ask your radio who did it." Ron said, "I'm sorry but the radio can't do that. It doesn't work that way." They said,

"But it tells you when the plane is coming and what's happening in La Paz. And it tells you what medicine to give people. This lady is really poor and she deserves your help." Ron said, "When I ask questions, I'm talking to a person who has another radio, and they answer my questions on their radio. The radio itself doesn't know who stole her cheeses." They repeated, "But she's so poor and she needs your help." They finally left, convinced we were very selfish with our magic tool. Others asked us to track down lost llamas or sheep.

The barometer was also considered magical, like the shamans' instruments. How else could it know when it was going to rain?

Our scariest magic item, however, was the tape recorder. Some thought it could *capture* anything anyone said, no matter where they were. Others thought it had a little man inside – or at least a man's talking head, since a whole person wouldn't fit.

Crossing the Mud River

January slipped by. Ron kept refining the alphabet, studying the grammar and memorizing vocabulary while I sketched items for our alphabet book. The rainy season weather was pleasant – warm in the sun and cool in the shade, with frequent rains. In February the rains kept falling until the Lauca River was too deep to cross. By the end of March, we had been in Chipaya almost five months. It was time for our annual mission conference at the jungle center, but we couldn't cross the rivers.

Then Ceferino suggested, "Maybe you could go out the back way where the rivers aren't as deep. The Rio Barras (Mud River) isn't too bad, except right after a hard rain." "But is there a road?" Ron asked. "I could show you the way." So after a couple sunny days, we decided to try it with Ceferino and another man to help push, pull, or whatever. It was a good thing because we needed them for all three before reaching Oruro.

At the first river, water ran into the Jeep but we made it across. For an hour and a half we crawled over sand dunes and spun through mud and water till we reached the Mud River. We waded the riverbed looking for the shallowest crossing, then made a run for it in low gear and four-wheel drive – only to sink in the muddy bank before we even got to the river! After unloading everything and carrying it across the river, Ron and his helpers jacked up the Jeep wheel by wheel, stuffing straw and shrubs under the tires until we could finally roll back out.

Fortunately there were lots of shrubs and large clumps of straw nearby to pave the bank and part of the river bed itself. Ron revved the motor and made it most of the way across. Clouds were gathering in the dark sky as he and the fellows worked in the river jacking up the Jeep again and putting more straw and shrubs under the wheels. Finally we got out – backwards to a shallow spot. More straw and shrubs, another run, and we finally made it out just as it started to rain. We said, "Thank You, Lord!" knowing there would soon be a flash flood. We reloaded the Jeep, grabbed a bite to eat, and were on our way again – after five and a half hours!

Suddenly the *road* dropped out from under us. Even the spare tire was in the mud. "More straw and shrubs!" An hour later we were on our way again. At dusk we were glad to find a schoolhouse to camp in for the night, sleeping on wooden benches. When I had cramps that night, I was glad for the river delays. If we had bumped along all day I probably would have lost the baby we were expecting. The tin roof turned our school house into a freezer before morning, so we were up and away by daybreak.

The next day our roads were more like dry plowed fields. At noon we reached another river which was narrow but too deep to ford, so we had to risk the bridge, even though a third of the planks had been stolen for firewood. We crept across inch by inch. Two or three times one back wheel was partly in mid air.

When we reached the Desaguadero River (*The Drain*), we learned that both barges had sunk, one with a truck on it. When a substitute barge arrived four and a half hours later, we finally crossed The Drain and bumped merrily along into Oruro where we stayed overnight with our friends. Our grand average for the two days was almost seven miles an hour!

The next day we drove down to Cochabamba, descending 7,000 feet in twenty-five miles. Ron had to hold the gearshift with one hand and the steering wheel with the other as he navigated the 180-degree turns on our one-lane road. What a relief to arrive safely at the mission house! Apparently, part of the Chipaya Challenge was to get there and get back all in one piece. Would it always be that bad?

Recess in the Jungle and the City

A couple weeks later we flew to Tumi Chucua, our mission center in the jungle, for conference. Since most language groups lived in the lowlands, this was headquarters for our director, most translators, teachers, nurses, and the JAARS pilots, mechanics, and radio technicians.

We enjoyed times of worship and sharing, business meetings and linguistic discussions. During conference hours, we ladies took turns caring for seven babies in the nursery. It was good to see everybody and catch up on all the news, as well as play volleyball and swim in the lake every evening.

Back in Cochabamba I hurried to finish trial copies of the Alphabet Book before Ron went to Chipaya for a couple months while I stayed in Cochabamba waiting for Debbie's playmate. During Ron's absence my main project was to type the 3,000 Chipaya words with their Spanish and English equivalents.

RON'S FIRST WINTER IN CHIPAYA

Ron had a harrowing, two-day trip by truck and bicycle from Oruro to Chipaya via Sabaya. So far, every trip had been a challenge.

In Chipaya, Ron lived simply, but it wasn't easy. Most meals were quinoa, often with carrots and onions. A couple times he washed clothes and baked bread. It was winter, but he didn't have enough kerosene to use the heater so many nights his feet never warmed up, making him wish he had taken a hot water bottle. In the morning it was 33 degrees in the house and barely warmed up to 42 degrees in the afternoon. After a week and a half, he caught a bad cold.

The two-way radio was his only link to the outside world. Lloyd Deister, our radio technician, had built a wind generator to recharge the truck battery that powered our transmitter, fastening a five-foot wooden propeller to a rubber wheel on a bicycle hub. Ron mounted and raised the propeller on a twenty-foot pole to catch the wind, estimating that four hours of wind would produce power for eight minutes of radio time.

For a week there was no wind and when it finally came, it was so strong the propeller spun too fast, vibrated too much and shook itself loose, stripping the threads on the screws that held it together. Ron lowered the propeller several times to fix different things until one day he heard it spinning so furiously he was afraid to go outside to look at it. Finally an extra strong gust of wind tore it off the pole, sending it crashing to the ground. Fortunately, no one was around to get hit. It was a good idea but the Chipaya winds were too much for it. So, instead of being able to chat with each other on the radio every few days, we were limited to a few minutes once a week.

Ron was hoping to work on the language with Ceferino, but when Ceferino dropped by he said, "Ever since I rode out to Oruro with you, the community has accused me of being a traitor and selling the language. They want to run me out of town."

Ron said, "Then I don't expect you to work with me here. Just be faithful to God. But do you think you could work with me in Cochabamba some time?" Ceferino said, "I'd like to do that."

The Hand-crank Phonograph

We were surprised when a box of records and a hand-crank phonograph came from Gospel Recordings in Los Angeles, California. A technician had helped Ceferino translate eight short Bible stories and messages into Chipaya after he became a Christian.

The phonograph was a novelty for the Chipayas and some days they cranked it for three or four hours, listening to stories of creation, Adam and Eve, the flood, the Ten Commandments, plus stories and teachings of Jesus. The story of the lost sheep was their favorite since they could all identify with the shepherd. Some days so many visitors came, Ron hardly had time to eat.

The school children liked the Alphabet Book, but the men said, "We already know what those objects are. These books must be for teaching others our language."

More Fiestas

On July 21, a series of fiestas started, including the celebration for Santa Ana, Chipaya's patron saint. Ceferino said West-Side and East-Side took turns being in charge of that fiesta, since the image belonged to both sides of town. Four men carried the image on a pedestal on their shoulders, her long dress flowing in the wind as they took her to visit four shrines at the corners of the church courtyard.

At sundown on July 30, three men ran down the road toward Escara, and three others ran toward Sabaya, to chase the *malos* (evil spirits) out of town.

On August 1, another series of fiestas ended the old ritual year and started the new one. At this time the community assigned families to be in charge of the dozens of fiestas for the coming year which included supplying the animal sacrifices, alcohol, coca leaves and a ritual meal for all the participants. As their population had been dwindling, the weight of these fiestas had become heavier and heavier, but they didn't dare neglect any of their spirit gods.

At this time the two mayors planted their *Father King* staffs by each home to protect it against sickness and harm for the following year, and took a few hairs from everybody's head for some other ritual. Ashes signaled where sacrifices and rituals had been performed.

A drunk man, slobbering a mouthful of coca leaves, came up to Ron, breathing in his face. He tried to explain everything to Ron, starting with Chipaya legends from before the time the sun appeared, but his slurred speech was such a garbled mixture of Chipaya, Aymara and Spanish that Ron couldn't understand much.

After all these fiestas they celebrated Bolivia's Independence Day, August 6, for a few more days.

With no language help, no generator to charge the radio battery and no kerosene for heat, Ron decided to leave earlier than planned.

Was it really only a year since we first reached Chipaya? So much had happened in twelve months! Whatever would the next year hold? Would it be easier? Harder? Only God knew and he wasn't telling.

Carla Kay Joins Us

Ron returned to Cochabamba in time to welcome Carla Kay into our family on August 15. She was so tiny she fit in Debbie's little doll buggy! Now Debbie, at fifteen months, suddenly seemed like a *big* girl.

The First Chipaya Books

A few days after Carla's arrival, Ceferino came to the city to work with Ron for a month. For initial translation practice they translated ten of Aesop's fables plus "The Little Red Hen" and a Chipaya folk tale. First Ron would tell Ceferino a story, they'd talk about how to adapt it to the Chipaya culture, then Ceferino would practice telling it in Chipaya, and finally they would record it. Then Ron transcribed the stories from the tape, we drew illustrations for them, and printed a booklet. At the same time we printed the Alphabet Book, hoping the Chipayas would enjoy these first booklets to ever be printed in their language. Ceferino also told about twenty short stories or incidents which Ron taped. We never dreamed how important these stories would be in analyzing the grammar of the language.

The fable that best fit the Chipaya culture was the story of the lazy donkey that kept sitting down in the river to lighten the load of salt he was carrying – till his master loaded him down with sponges.

Ron and Ceferino substituted wool for sponges then only the names of the places needed to be changed. One day, back in Chipaya, when a lot of people were in town, Ron read the stories to a small crowd lounging in the sand behind our house. When he finished, an old grandma said, "Those stories must *really* be old! I don't even remember hearing them before."

Aesop's fables had suddenly become Chipaya legends!

3

THE FIRST TO MEET HIM
1962-1964

THE SECOND RAINY SEASON

A TERRIBLE YET WONDERFUL YEAR

On our next trip to Chipaya, with Debbie and baby Carla, we hired a truck. Besides our food supplies, we took a couple barrels of kerosene and some lumber.

The lumber was to build a sleeping loft above our kitchen/dining room. Dirt and dust filled our house again for a few days while they dug holes in our adobe walls for the joists to support the loft. A sturdy ladder served for stairs. The loft was almost six feet high on the plaza side, down to nothing on the opposite side. Ron also chopped a hole for a window overlooking the plaza. Our new bedroom was roomy, private, and wonderful! Ten-foot wide construction plastic was perfect for stapling to the rafters as a ceiling to keep dirt and sand from the straw roof from sifting onto our pillows and blankets.

Since the wind generator hadn't worked, Lloyd Deister had arranged a packet of solar cells to recharge our two-way radio battery. It worked great. We had sunshine every day, sometimes for twelve hours, so now we could have regular radio schedules with co-workers and nurses, and even had enough power for a bicycle headlight to light our new bedroom.

We had been hoping for at least one more couple to join Ceferino and his wife who had been the only Christians for two and a half years, but when we saw Ceferino, he said, "They want to throw me out of town! They say I'm a hindrance because I use the water and pasture but never help with the sacrifices and rituals. And they say, 'Becoming a believer might be contagious – like the plague,' so they won't have anything to do with me." Our hearts sank.

A Girlfriend's Curse

The week before we had left Cochabamba, a very sick, penniless man had showed up in the outskirts of the city asking for a *gringo* named Ronaldo. He wouldn't give his name, but when he finally admitted he was from Chipaya, the missionaries called us.

Eugene had been beaten up in a drunken brawl in Chipaya, and the shamans divined he was going to die because an old girlfriend had cursed him. He had come to the city to see an herb doctor, but ended up worse and penniless. Ron arranged housing and meals for him, talked to him about a loving and powerful God, and arranged for him to travel back to Chipaya.

When Eugene reached Chipaya, sick and weak, Job's comforters gathered around saying "It's too bad you're going to die! We're sorry but there's nothing anyone can do about it." Only Ron gave him hope, saying, "God is stronger than the spirits, and stronger than anyone's curse. Why don't you *enter God's Way* and ask Him to heal you? Then, even if you die, you'll go to God's town in heaven."

The Curse is Broken

Back in Chipaya, Eugene borrowed the Chipaya Gospel records plus some Aymara and Spanish records to play for his wife and two boys, and he had long talks with Ceferino who lived nearby. For a couple weeks he weighed his options, though in a sense he had nothing to lose because everyone expected him to die, anyway. Finally he decided to enter God's Way. At first his wife was angry and accused him of adultery, but the judge threatened to fine *her* for such a ridiculous accusation! A few days later she, too, decided to enter God's way. The number of believers had suddenly doubled! It was wonderful!

The whole town watched as Eugene recovered bit by bit. A few said, "Maybe God *is* stronger!" Then the shamans became alarmed and stirred up the Chipayas against Ceferino and Eugene for leaving the old ways. They insisted, "You *can't* be a Christian *and* a Chipaya."

As opposition mounted, Maxine's husband, Tomas, forbade her to visit us. Since he was a shaman, we weren't surprised but I missed her help and her friendship, and no one else ever took her place in my Laundromat.

For Sale: The Original Language

Chipaya legends say they were the original people, so of course their language was the original one. They were among the first inhabitants of the *altiplano*, even predating the Incas. For two and a half centuries the Chipayas and Aymaras had disputed the land using the Spanish and Aymara languages, with no outsider ever trying to learn Chipaya.

So they kept asking us, "Why do you want to learn our language?" We said, "To write it down, teach you to read, and translate God's Book." They didn't buy that. Surely we had some ulterior motive. They concluded the world had suddenly discovered the worth of their original language and we had come to steal it and sell it for a fortune – leaving them with no language to speak. Or maybe the U.S. wanted it for a secret code language during war time.

We had printed the Alphabet Book to show their language *could* be written, but Ramon announced, "They're selling these books all over Oruro!" as proof that we were selling the language. So the Chipaya authorities declared, "Anyone who helps them learn the language is betraying Chipaya!" Getting language help looked utterly hopeless now. The Chipayas no longer talked freely around us and when Ron tried to talk to them, they would clam up or walk away. It was very discouraging.

Actually, they didn't trust any outsiders: Aymaras tried to steal their land; the government didn't help them; Spanish speakers looked down on them and foreigners came to take pictures and make money off of them. They felt frustrated and hemmed in, with a smoldering resentment against everything foreign. And we were foreigners.

We had hoped for more language help when there were more believers, but it didn't happen. Ron said, "If they're persecuted it needs to be for following Christ, not for helping us."

How Could We Win Friends?

As outsiders in a closed society, our most important job, obviously, was to try to make friends by helping them in whatever way they needed.

Shortly after we first arrived, the mayor announced, "Aymaras are planting quinoa on our land. Please drive out and take pictures of them as proof." They didn't actually have a word for "please," but their intonation sometimes gave a hint of it. The next day both mayors said, "Please go with us to plant quinoa on our land then drive us to La Paz in your Jeep to present our case to the President." Ron said, "I'll go with you to plant quinoa and I'll help pay your truck fares to La Paz but I can't drive you there."

When we had the Jeep, the Chipayas were always asking him to run errands for them. Of course this was much easier for them than peddling their bikes. Sometimes he got tired of being their errand boy.

Ron also spent many hours typing old hand-written documents concerning their land problems. At times they brought several pages, expecting him to drop everything and type them immediately and if he said he couldn't, they'd say, "Ah, what good is the gringo, anyway?" Providing them with their own typewriters a year or so later was a big help for them and for us.

One day Ron spent all morning discussing land problems with town officials. After our director set up a court appearance for them in La Paz, we wondered if they would actually go. Ron kept telling them, "You need to arrive in La Paz at least two days ahead of schedule to meet the Minister of Rural Affairs." But we never knew what they would do. One fellow said, "If the government doesn't keep the Aymaras off our land, we aren't going to be part of anything, not even Bolivia. We'll just be independent."

Whenever possible, Ron joined in community work, even though it sometimes backfired. After working several hours to help divert the river, there was a small leak in the earth dam. He heard them mutter, "It's *his* fault. He scared the water spirits. Why did he come, anyway?" We were thankful when the leak stopped.

Maybe our being there in collaboration with the government brought out the *gimme* syndrome. They felt we were taking something from them and should give something in return. They didn't like to pay for medicines, either, yet they'd pay any price the shaman named.

Besides the bicycle parts, everyone appreciated our bringing barrels of kerosene from Oruro to sell, because they couldn't transport them on their bicycles. Every day folks came with their bottles to buy a bit of kerosene to start their cooking fires or for the one-watt kerosene wick lamps Ron fashioned for them from baby food jars. He made forty the very first month and many more in the following months.

The Chipayas liked it when Ron helped roof their houses because he was tall enough to hand the straw to those working up on the roof.

Chipaya town houses had always been in clusters, but now they were mapping out streets from the corners of the plaza. Ron spent one day carrying sod blocks on his bicycle to help the mayor build a new round house after tearing down his old one which was in the way of the new street. At the same time they decided that all houses facing the plaza should be rectangular.

Ron loaned his saw and hammer and smoothed many a weaving stick with his plane. He often loaned his tools, although Eulogio was the only one who ever returned them on his own. When he loaned them to anyone else, he had to hunt them down.

One day Ramon, our antagonist, started building the stand for a flag pole in the middle of the plaza. He carried stones and a bit of cement, gathered sand, and carried water. When Ron saw him working alone, he offered to help and in a couple days they finished the project. Ramon didn't criticize us quite so loudly after that.

Children didn't have many toys other than rag balls to kick around, but they managed to have fun with lambs or piglets, and homemade kites. They really liked the *cars* Ron made for them by nailing four tin can lids to a scrap of wood. In one month alone he made forty of them. One day he helped several boys fix the *noses* of their tops.

At the same time, I helped dozens of girls and boys sew rag dolls which they stuffed with wool. I used markers to draw dark eyes and a red smile. After staring at me for a while, one little girl said, "*Her* lips *are* red, aren't they?" Then I noticed their lips just looked dark brown. Another day when our front room was full of children sewing dolls and two girls were sitting on the floor under my desk, I heard the older girl say, "Put the needle in at the north, pull it out at the south and keep the thread on the west." Living on the high, barren plains with only the sun and the distant mountains to orient them, all directions were given using the cardinal directions, never saying right or left. It was several years before we realized our world map was hanging on the wrong wall: the east side of the map was toward the west!

The school children enjoyed looking at *National Geographic Magazines* and making twenty-four or forty-eight piece puzzles in our front room. When our daughters were older, they played jump rope and other games with them in the plaza.

For the young men, we brought a basketball and hoop to put on a backboard. They enjoyed playing though their game was a combination of basketball and soccer! The school children enjoyed the basketball as well but the authorities grumbled about the dirty marks on the new school wall.

The Advantage of a Hard Head

I tried not to be hard headed, but one time it paid off.

Early one morning when Carla woke up crying for a bottle, I wrapped her in a blanket and headed sleepily for the ladder so she wouldn't wake Debbie. Holding her in my left arm, I stepped down to the top rung and reached with my right hand for the two-by-four hand rail – but missed – plunging head first to the stone floor. Fortunately I turned as I fell, so Carla wasn't crushed. Ron woke with a start and scrambled down the ladder to help us. The inch-thick pavestone had radial cracks and my skull probably did, too, but other than a bad headache for a week or two, I was okay. It could have been much worse.

Shortly after that, Carla got sick. On Tuesday she just had a little cold. Wednesday she started coughing and by night she had a deep, hard, dry cough. Thursday she was so hoarse she couldn't even cry. It reminded us of the time Debbie was so sick. We gave her all the medicine we had and by radio we asked our co-workers in the jungle and the city to pray for her. That night she slept well and Friday she was much better. We were so thankful!

More Believers!

Zenobio had heard the Gospel while working on a Seventh Day Adventist's farm in Chile. When his oldest son was very sick, he asked the shaman, "Why is he so sick?" The shaman said, "The spirits are demanding that you sacrifice five sheep, or else they'll eat your son's spirit and he'll die." So Zenobio killed five sheep and sprinkled the blood on the ground to the spirits. The next day his son was no better so he inquired again, "What more do the spirits want?" "Five more sacrifices!" said the shaman. So he sacrificed five more. The third day the shaman said, "They still demand *five more* sacrifices!" Desperate to save his son's life, Zenobio sacrificed five more sheep, although it almost wiped out his small flock – fifteen sheep for the life of his son – and the next day his son died. Distraught, angry and hopeless, the grieving father vowed, "I'm through serving the spirits!"

Zenobio's brother-in-law, Eulogio, had listened to the Bible story records many times, and in January the two men visited Ron. After hearing Zenobio's story, Ron said, "The True God is not like the spirits you worship. Instead of demanding sacrifices, he loves us so much he sent his own Son, Jesus, to die for our sins, so we could become his children." After reading verses from the Spanish Bible, Ron gave them each copies of Mark and Luke in simple Spanish. He said, "If you'll read these with your wives at home, they'll help you understand what God is like."

By the end of January both couples had determined to enter God's Way. Now there were four Christian couples. The number of believers had doubled again! We were thrilled!

Zenobio was a strong character. When the community chose him to be Mayor, he said, "Okay, but I'll never make sacrifices or serve coca or alcohol." Surprisingly, the community agreed. Instead of throwing a big drinking party to celebrate his appointment, Zenobio invited the believers to his country home to sing, pray and enjoy a meal. It was the first time he had ever killed a sheep just for food rather than as a sacrifice.

The community was furious and demanded that Zenobio and Eulogio return to the old ways or else...

As the new believers discussed the community threats, Zenobio said, "I don't care what they do to me. They can kill my body, but not my soul. I'm through being ordered around by Satan. Let them kill me – I'm a believer now and if they kill me I'll go to be with God. That is better anyway!"

Eulogio, on the other hand, was a timid, kindly person – "like a lily in a mud-hole," as Ron said. A couple weeks after entering God's Way, he met his brother-in-law, Antonio, who was raving mad, saying, "You've made a terrible mistake! Why are you leaving the old ways? You're no longer a Chipaya! I'm going to stir up the community against you. I'm going to make sure all your flocks are confiscated, and your wife and little children are taken away, and you get thrown out of town. It's easy to do this. The wife and children of a believer *can* be taken away from them!" He ended his tirade calling Eulogio all kinds of horrible names. Devastated, Eulogio walked back to town to ask Ron, "Is it true they can take away my family and my flocks?" Ron said, "No, not legally. There's freedom of religion in Bolivia, but it's hard to know what they might do." It made us angry that Satan was picking on the weakest person.

Because of the animosity and threats against them, the believers met in their country homes at night. When they asked what the Bible taught about many different topics, Ron had them read relevant passages from the Spanish Bible. One Sunday the men rode their bicycles about eight miles to worship with an Aymara family.

The believers decided to take turns meeting in their country homes on Tuesdays, Fridays and Sundays. (Might it have been because Tuesdays and Fridays were *bad days* when evil spirits prowled around?) We suggested studying simple correspondence lessons from an Indian Bible Institute in Cochabamba, so the next Friday they met at Eulogio's West-Side home to study the first lesson. That day Ceferino happened to come late because he was keeping sheep and llamas out of the quinoa plots, and another man was absent because the Aymaras' donkeys were eating his quinoa.

"Did He *really* come alive again?"

Ron tried to figure out the grammar rules by studying the Gospel records, Aesop's Fables, and short stories folks had recorded for the novelty of hearing their voice on tape.

I continued writing mini stories about Jesus in Spanish and searching for a picture to illustrate each one. We did a mock-up of a booklet and titled it "About Easter" because that is a big holiday in all of Latin America. We showed it to folks who dropped in, hoping someone would help us translate it.

Another month slipped by with no language help until finally, one Sunday afternoon in February, Ceferino helped Ron translate some of the Easter story.

Then one day, in spite of the edict against helping us, two men happened by and stayed all day to help transcribe the Gospel stories on the records and the next day they came again to translate the rest of the Easter story. In two days we had fourteen hours of language help – almost as much as in the previous five months! It was wonderful!

Now when folks came around, we could read the stories to them in their own language. When one man finished reading the whole Easter booklet he said, "I thought they killed Jesus because he was so wicked. Did he really come alive again? *For real*?"

We said, "Yes. For real!"

Cursed!

In February, 1963, the rain kept falling till the rivers in the north overflowed large areas of the plains, flowing slowly toward the salt flats in the southwest. Soon a river ran alongside and across the airstrip, our supposed emergency exit route. A couple days later the town plaza was a lake. We saw men wading through town with their pant-legs rolled up or with their trousers folded up under their arms!

The rain destroyed much of the quinoa crop, which was almost ready to harvest. It flooded the sheep and llamas' grazing grounds, so animals were starving. Llama dung, the Chipayas' basic cooking fuel, was soaked. Some homes were flooded. The frantic shamans desperately ordered sacrifices and more sacrifices to the water spirits, wondering who was to blame for the flood. Which of their spirit gods were demanding sacrifices?

The flood water came within ten feet of our front door and twenty of our back door. Our outhouse caved in just as Ron was about to use it!

The Carnival (Mardi Gras) fiesta was spoiled. Tuesday morning Herman came to buy kerosene. Ron filled his bottle from the kitchen barrel and the man left. As he exited another man entered, and Ron noticed blood on the floor where Herman had stood. Ron knew what it meant, but he asked, "What does that mean?" The man muttered, "For working an evil," and quickly left. Obviously, a sacrifice had been made to put a curse on us. We didn't know if it was because of the flood or because three couples had recently become Christians.

The next few days, people stared at us to see if the curse was taking effect. When Ron walked around town some folks laughed in his face. The atmosphere felt eerie and evil. We prayed for God to protect us.

On Wednesday Ron dumped our pot of waste a little way out of town. Later he saw a man bent over the spot, with his hat off. The only times they took off their felt hats was when they slept or performed rituals. Clearly he was trying to put a hex on us but we couldn't blame the Chipayas for cursing us in an effort to save themselves.

About five o'clock the next morning, our house shook. The wall of the Catholic chapel, about thirty feet from our house, had collapsed, taking the worship center with it. As a crowd gathered, a little boy remarked, "Jesus Christ was in there," assuming he must not have much power if he let the wall cave in on him.

Ron said, "No, Jesus Christ is in heaven. That was just a picture of Him."

Later in the morning as Ron helped the men salvage the objects in the chapel plus the doors, windows and rafters, the water went down dramatically. He heard the men say, "The water came up and got the priest's house, then receded. The priest must be to blame!"

Regardless of their reasoning, we were thankful they no longer blamed us for the flood.

When the men saw a set of large Bible pictures in the Catholic chapel, they asked, "What's that?"

Ron said, "They're pictures of Jesus from the Bible. Want me to tell you about them?"

They said, "Sure."

So he said, "Come to our house and I'll tell you the stories." Five or six men listened to Bible stories for almost half an hour that day.

A few days later the water rose higher than ever, but we never felt the blame of the community again.

"String him up!"

The most frightening thing, however, happened about a week later. We heard loud banging on our front door, and angry voices of drunken men speaking Aymara. We hoped they would just go away, but they kept banging and hollering, "String him up! He has no business being here! String him up!"

Ron finally whispered, "I don't want them to break the door down but I can't let them in the house. There's no telling what they'd do. I'm going out to talk to them. Latch the door behind me so they can't push their way in." Then he opened the door just enough to slip out. The hardest thing I ever did was lock the door behind him. What would they do to him? What would *I* do if they harmed him? I dropped to my knees on the stone floor by the adobe bench, with baby Carla in one arm, and my other arm around Debbie, crying to the Lord to protect Ron.

Between the men's yells, I could hear Ron trying to reason with them in a low voice. Finally one man muttered, "Oh, come on. Leave them be, or we'll never get to Sabaya." With that they turned and waded off across the flooded plaza, mumbling and grumbling as they went.

Then Ron tapped lightly on the door saying, "You can open the door now. They're gone."

Once inside, he picked up Debbie, and I cried as we stood hugging each other and thanking God for his protection.

Ron explained, "They're angry because they can't drive home to Sabaya to celebrate Mardi Gras. They still have miles to go. The man who talked them into leaving was the truck driver who brought our supplies."

Threats and Responses

Next the desperate community turned its anger on the new believers, threatening, "We're going to kill all of you, confiscate your flocks and destroy your houses if you don't help us placate the spirits!" We didn't think they would actually kill them, but if they got riled up when they were drunk, there was no telling what they might do. We prayed for their protection and prayed that the opposition would strengthen their commitment to follow God, rather than make them cave in. If the new Christian church was to survive, these first believers had to be strong, whether we were present or not.

Sunday, when Ron met with the believers in Zenobio's country home, they said, "Everybody has been watching us, making fun of us, waiting for calamity to strike us for leaving the old ways. But we're all okay." Zenobio said, "My baby doesn't cry so much." And Eulogio's wife, Petrona, said, "My baby hasn't had convulsions." They added, "Eugene used to be afraid of dying, but now he's at peace, even though he's still sick. We need to be firm."

They read a lot of verses about God's care.

A Bride's Price

Agustin was not a strong character like his brother Zenobio. Being rather unkempt and sloppy, he hadn't been able to find a wife. However, after one of the fiestas, a lady named Gregoria got herself locked up with a fine on her head for "enticing married men to sleep with her." Since she couldn't pay her fine, the judge said, "Whoever pays her fine can have her as his wife!" So Agustin paid the bride's price and had a wife! Although he wanted to enter God's Way, he was afraid to because his new wife wasn't in agreement, his parents threatened to take his flocks, and of course the whole community was against him. But his brother Zenobio and the other believers encouraged him, and finally he, too, entered God's Way.

That week the water came within five feet of our front door and ten feet of our back door. On some parts of the airstrip the water was well above Ron's knees. Our mission conference time was approaching but our chances of flying out in March were nil.

March 9, Ron's birthday, we woke up hearing water lapping at our north wall. Ron jumped up to build a dike. The cold water made his feet and legs ache but fortunately, when Zenobio came to buy kerosene, he got his shovel and helped build the dike. Eighteen houses in town and over seventy country homes had already collapsed, besides innumerable corrals. Fortunately our house was on higher ground, with some rocks in the above-ground foundation.

Several men came by that morning, and as always the subject turned to the water. The mayor commented, "It must be a punishment." Ron agreed, "Yes, God is calling to Chipaya, 'Come to Me. Come to Me.'" The new mayor said, "Please pray to your God to take away the water." Ron replied, "Maybe God is sending it for a purpose – calling Chipaya to stop serving the spirits and the ancestors and to follow him alone. He *could* take away all this water." The mayor didn't respond as his main duty was to lead the rituals for placating all the spirits.

That same day the community dug up ten or twelve skulls from under the old church. They placed them in front of the big altar and prayed to them, sacrificed a sheep, sprinkled them with the blood, and burned incense. The following Saturday they buried them again.

Finally in mid-March the water subsided, leaving a thick blanket of mud on the airstrip.

On March 19, we invited the believers for our going away meal, though we didn't know when we would be able to leave. We included Gregoria, Agustin's wife, and Fortunato, a single man, who said he wanted to follow God. Everyone enjoyed the meal which included four gallons of quinoa soup, sixty small potatoes, most of an eighteen-pound sheep, sixty-five muffins and a kettle of coffee!

That night, Gregoria and Fortunato both entered God's Way, bringing the total number of believers to eleven. We had prayed for two more Christians and now there were nine more! We also heard that Maximo planned to join the group as soon as he fulfilled his civic responsibility.

Encouraged by their larger group, the believers met in town by daylight on Sunday from one o'clock till five. Besides reading Scripture and singing in Spanish they had long discussions in Chipaya and organized officially as a church, choosing Ceferino as the leader and Eulogio as treasurer. We were amazed by Eugene's Bible knowledge simply gained by reading his Bible a lot, since he was basically bedridden.

When the believers met again, Maximo had completed his community service. Ceferino explained the Gospel to him and his wife, Vicenta, and helped them pray to enter God's Way, bringing the number of believers to thirteen. We could hardly believe it! God was doing amazing things!

A Bicycle Taxi and The Everlasting Arms

The rivers were too deep, the *altiplano* too muddy for truck travel, and our airstrip was deep in mud. When the Chipayas told Ron about a long, smooth salt flat which seemed ideal for an airstrip, Ron passed the news to our mission pilots in the jungle. The only trouble was that this landing strip was ten miles and seven rivers away, and I couldn't ride a man's bike. But in the nick of time, our friend Pastor Napoleon peddled into Chipaya and offered to be my taxi driver. The day before our scheduled flight, Ron peddled to the airstrip to check and mark the runway, and calculate the direction from the Escara Mountain, using his compass.

A teacher was going to stay in our house while we were away so we didn't need to lock everything up.

Our JAARS pilot would be flying from our mission center and stopping to refuel in a jungle town before climbing 8,500 feet to Cochabamba. After that four-hour flight, it would take him two hours to scale the Andes and land on the *altiplano* at 12,000 feet. Our flight from Chipaya back to Cochabamba would be another two hours.

As we left the house that morning, we could see clouds up north. Ron rode his bicycle, Pastor Napoleon tied a small woolen blanket around the bar of his bike for me to sit side saddle, and believers with bicycles carried Debbie, Carla and the two-way radio on their backs. Others carried our bags, drinking water and homemade bread for lunch on their bicycle racks while others, including Tomas the shaman, just rode along out of curiosity.

Our bicycle caravan wended its way over llama trails, sandy and muddy stretches, and through seven rivers. Five were shallow, but two were so deep even Ron had to carry his trousers. I pulled my skirt as high as I could, and at the deepest hole, I climbed on Ron's back! Fortunately by then it was almost noon so the rivers weren't so cold.

We reached the salt flat in three hours. It was amazingly smooth, wide and long, with a river to one side. Debbie was happy to be on solid ground again, and I was tremendously thankful for Napoleon's strong legs that peddled me all that way. Ron stretched out a long antenna wire for the radio so he could talk to the pilot.

By then it was past noon. The wind had picked up and dark clouds were getting close. We needed to beat the rain. We shared our bread with those who had carried our things, and waited for the plane, straining to be first to see and hear it. Before long it approached, flew over the salt flat once, circled, landed, and taxied back to us.

As the propeller stopped, everyone crowded around the Cessna. The pilot, Bill Key, offered to take three Chipayas on a short flight as a trial take-off, in appreciation for carrying our things. They were trembling with excitement as they climbed in and buckled up. Bill taxied to the end of the runway, revved the motor and sped down the runway. We expected the plane to rise quickly but it barely got off the ground at the end of the salt flat. We held our breath as it wavered up and down then landed between two forks of the river. Ron jumped on his bicycle to ride over to it. The Chipayas were delighted with their flight, never dreaming it was meant to be much higher and longer.

Bill checked the engine and cleaned the sparkplugs. All he could imagine was that he had gotten dirty gas when he refueled in the jungle. In the meantime, the storm blew in and rained on us. Now what? How could he even get the plane back to the salt flat? The sandy strip between the rivers was short and the strong wind was blowing the wrong direction. As Bill and Ron prayed, suddenly the wind shifted. Bill revved the motor and the wind was just enough to get him off the ground and back to the long salt flat, where the rest of us were waiting. Ron rode back on his bicycle.

By then it was 4:30 in the afternoon and raining lightly. What should we do? Would we be able to fly with all of us and our baggage, little as it was? We would have to leave right away to reach Cochabamba before dark, otherwise we would have to make the three-hour trip back to Chipaya for the night. And what would the pilot do? He couldn't leave the plane overnight. We finally decided to load up and try to fly. Just then the wind changed again to blow in the right direction for lift-off. We waved a quick goodbye to the Chipayas and prayed as Bill revved the motor.

Using all the emergency measures, we barely lifted off at the end of the long salt flat. Fortunately, there weren't any trees or even shrubs to clear. The verse that kept playing in my mind was, "...and underneath are the Everlasting Arms. Underneath are the Everlasting Arms" (Deut. 33:27). We were all too busy praying to talk.

Bit by bit we inched higher above the rivers, mud flats and sand dunes. Would we get enough altitude in an hour to cross the Andes? As we approached the mountains, Bill spotted the lowest pass, and we slipped through with the mountains rising higher on either side. I lifted my feet to keep them from dragging! Finally, at dusk, we landed in Cochabamba, whispering, "Thank you, Lord, for your Everlasting Arms!"

So ended our second rainy season in Chipaya. It had been a tough, frustrating time, but now there were thirteen believers instead of two. It had been a terrible yet wonderful year!

Now it was time to fly down to the jungle for conference then back to Cochabamba to wait for another little Olson to join our family.

Ron's Second Winter in Chipaya

New Believers Tested by Fire

In July, Eugene and his family came to Cochabamba again for medical help. He said, "The believers are suffering. The community took them to the police in Sabaya to imprison them or kick them out of Chipaya, but the police said, 'We can't do either of those things because there's freedom of religion in Bolivia.' Then the community resorted to threats and abuses, saying they won't give us land to plant our quinoa. All those who were interested in the Gospel have been scared away."

When Ron went to Chipaya for a month of winter, he did *not* get a warm welcome. The teacher had used up all our kerosene and flour, and left our house in a mess. Our neighbor, Francisco, Mateo's father, had promised to save kerosene for us, but his wife said, "Sorry. There isn't any." By the time Ron got some, it was afternoon, and he was really hungry, as he hadn't had much to eat on the trip out the previous day.

Ceferino confirmed Eugene's bad news and added, "When we men are away they try to molest our wives, and they even raped Victoria, my seven-year-old daughter. My wife wants to move away from Chipaya. When Eugene's wife returned from the city, her mother-in-law asked her to help cook a meal. As she was helping cook, several women closed in on her, forcing her to drink alcohol and chew coca – symbols of worshipping the spirits. Her brother Juan wanted to become a believer, but late one night the authorities ordered him to appear at a community meeting where the men grabbed him by the throat, picked up stones, and forced him to agree to take charge of a fiesta, including the sacrifices and rituals."

The believers told Ron, "After you flew out in March, Tomas bragged, 'You don't have to worry about them anymore. I cursed the plane so they're going to crash and all be killed!'"

Maximo added, "After you left, a priest and nun visited all the believers. They said, 'You should ask the bishop if you're on the right road. If he agrees you are, that's fine, but if not, you should be good Catholics again.' The nun asked me, 'Why are you supporting the *gringo*?' I said, 'I'm not supporting the *gringo*. I'm supporting God, and he is, too.' She asked, 'What will he give you?' I said, 'Nothing.' She said, 'We could give you food and clothes and other goods.' I said, 'I have enough.' Finally I said, 'You believe the Bible and we believe the Bible. What more is there to talk about?'" Then they left.

Later in the day Zenobio admitted, "We haven't been meeting regularly because Ceferino is usually away on weekends, and hasn't organized meetings. Most of the believers are confused and don't know which way to turn. Ceferino is sort of a coward and that's why people pick on him. They leave me alone. Some believers are wondering if they should move away, but where would they go?"

Zenobio paused then added sadly, "My baby died." Another pause. "And a couple weeks ago, three of my relatives died. They got a fever and started coughing up blood, and died in just a few days. After one of them died, his sick wife came to Eulogio's house before daybreak, saying, 'Whether I live or die, I want to enter God's Way.' Eulogio called the believers and Ceferino helped her pray to be saved. We met again later in the day to teach her more, but just after sundown she died. We sang and prayed till about midnight, then carried her body to her house so her family could perform whatever rituals they wanted."

Zenobio was silent for a while then smiled. "That night I dreamed well. I was asking the lady who died about heaven. She said, 'I had to pass three checkpoints before reaching God. Some believers have gold or copper houses. Mine is silver, but I'm fine. The unbelievers are suffering terribly.' I wanted to ask more questions but then I woke up."

Ron said, "Nowadays God usually speaks to us through the Bible, but in Bible times he often spoke to people in dreams."

Maximo's aunt and uncle, who had raised him when his parents died, were furious that he left the old ways. His aunt shouted, "We belong to Satan's party, and you shouldn't leave the old ways." When she was drunk during a fiesta, she barged into his house and knocked the soup bowl out of his hands, raving at him the whole time. When he finally got her to leave, she stumbled home and fell asleep. A bit later she woke up, crawling around on the floor, muttering incoherently. Her husband called the authorities, saying, "Maximo cursed my wife and now she's out of her head!" The authorities commanded Maximo, "Cure her!" He didn't know what to do, but finally brewed an herb tea for her, and eventually she fell asleep again.

Another night this same aunt and uncle railed against Maximo saying, "We're going to run you out of town! Or beat you to death! And we don't even care if we go to jail for it!" Maximo told Ron, "They made my wife cry. All my family is against me, but in my heart I know it's right to follow God and I'll never go back to the old ways." Ron reminded him about what Jesus, Peter and Paul suffered, and about the assurance we have of eternal life in heaven.

Heaven was a precious hope for the Chipayas, whose life was a constant struggle. Several believers said, "We wish we could go to heaven right now!"

Small Rays of Light

Since no one was buying the alphabet books, Ron gave one to each of the ninety-three school children. They were delighted since the only books they had were notebooks for copying lessons from the blackboard.

Several families borrowed the Gospel records to listen to them secretly in their country homes, and on two occasions a fellow told Ron how to say something in Chipaya. That was very encouraging because it had never happened before. When the priests encouraged the community to rebuild the Catholic Church which had crumbled years before, West-Side decided to build a big church close to the bell tower. The community leaders told the believers, "It's community work and you have to help." After considering it, the believers said, "Since it is town work we will help build it, but we won't take part in any of the rituals or in worshipping the idols or the evil spirits." Surprised by their agreeing to help, the community reconsidered their demand. That night, some of the shamans had bad dreams. In the morning they said, "The spirits must not want the Christians to be involved," so they told the believers, "You can make adobes for the school instead." The believers said, "Gladly," and were thankful they didn't have to help build the church which was Catholic in name but pagan in usage.

After batching it for a month, Ron stayed in Chipaya to celebrate Bolivia's Independence Day. He shot off rockets and firecrackers he had brought from Cochabamba, gave prizes to school children for winning races, and distributed five pounds of hard candy. Zenobio said, "Everybody really liked that!"

After the festivities, Ron peddled to Escara and caught a truck back to civilization.

Barbie Joy Arrives

While Ron was in Chipaya, the girls and I stayed in Cochabamba where I spent a lot of time in the print shop tracing pictures for our Easter book, then working on stories from Genesis.

Ron returned just in time for Carla's first birthday on August 15, and on September 10 Barbie Joy arrived – and she was a joy!

Language Work and Linguistics

Ceferino came to Cochabamba to work with Ron again for a few weeks. Then near the end of October, Ron flew to Mexico to work with Dr. Robert Longacre, a comparative linguist, to investigate whether or not Chipaya was related to the Maya languages, as a consultant had suggested the previous year. Their studies, published in the *International Journal of American Linguistics,*[3] seemed to indicate that Chipaya, or maybe a block of South American Indian languages, were related to Maya.

THE THIRD RAINY SEASON CUT SHORT

Continued Persecution

Since rivers were deep again by the time Ron returned from Mexico in late December, we were thankful the new JAARS plane, a Helio Courier, could fly us and our three little girls to Chipaya on January 4.

We had heard the believers were stoned and beaten in November for trying to have a street meeting. We admired their boldness but wished they'd be more tactful.

Back in Chipaya, things seemed calm until we heard Eugene's story. He said, "An evangelist from Chile wanted to preach in Chipaya, so while the community was building the Catholic Church, some believers accompanied him to the plaza where they sang a bit and the evangelist started preaching. The angry builders threw stones then rushed at them. Egged on by Vicente, a major shaman, they caught the preacher, tore his clothes, beat and kicked him, and threw him bodily out of town. Three or four men on bicycles chased Zenobio till they caught him and treated him the same way while others followed Eulogio and beat him."

Then, like in Bible times, they hunted down all the believers, beat them and confiscated their Bibles and songbooks, threatening to destroy their houses, steal their sheep, and throw them out of town if they didn't recant. Eugene finally gave in and said, "Okay, I'll stop following God." Ceferino took off, leaving his wife to bear the brunt of it. Fortunato renounced the Gospel and Eulogio was forced to work on the Catholic Church. Everyone was still riled up when we arrived six weeks later.

Ron encouraged the believers to be true to the Lord and not retaliate, reminding them how the early Christians were persecuted. But he also radioed Dave Farah for documents from La Paz guaranteeing religious freedom.

In spite of the opposition, a few brave folks said, "We're thinking about entering God's Way, but we'll wait to see if it's *legal*, and if the believers *win*."

Since the Easter Book was printed, I showed and read it to whoever would look and listen.

Medicine for Having Babies

As usual, sick folk came for medicine. One man had symptoms of hepatitis. Another man said, "My wife wants medicine for having babies. We've been married five years and don't have any children." Ron said, "I'm sorry. There's no medicine for that." The man said, "Your wife has had three babies in three years. You *must* have some medicine." Ron repeated, "I'm sorry, we don't." The man begged, "Please, Tall Brother. We want children so badly!"

How could we convince him?

Yunguyo's Curse

Whenever there was lightning or thunder, we unplugged the antenna wire from the radio and hung it on a big nail in the wall. The girls liked to watch sparks dance and jump from the end of it, but it scared the Chipayas. We were thankful for the lightning rod on our antenna pole.

By early February, Ron felt tired, a bit nauseous, and ached all over but he kept working on the grammar and visiting with whoever came.

Then on February 14, lightning struck a house in town not far from our house, burning a hole in the sod wall near the top of the door and cutting a jagged path to the ground. A crowd gathered quickly, standing at a safe distance, talking excitedly in low tones affirming that "The apostles shot their flaming arrows at the demons in the house!" Now the house was taboo, and the first to enter would be killed or struck blind. The family wanted to salvage their possessions, but even the powerful shamans were afraid to enter.

Then they spotted Ron. Didn't he say his God was stronger than the evil spirits? Let him take the curse! So they asked him, "Tall Brother, will you go in and bring out their belongings?" Ron said, "Yes. God is more powerful than the demons." Then he opened the door and stepped over the threshold as the Chipayas watched with bated breath. Only after Ron carried out some clothes and cooking pots did a shaman cautiously step inside, swinging his incense bowl, muttering incantations. Then he, too, picked up clothes and other items, piling them on the ground outside, to be *cleansed* by more rituals. Slowly the crowd dispersed.

Later that week, the believers met in our house, squinting as they entered the bright lamplight. They said, "We've wanted a place to meet in town. Maybe we could buy the house struck by lightning. The owners won't want to live in it." Someone added, "Maybe it will remind them God is stronger than the spirits." They told Zenobio, "Talk to the owner since he's your relative."

We were glad to see their faith in God. Happily, they sang all ten Chipaya songs then Ron read verses from the Spanish Bible about God's power and protection. They discussed the verses then explained them in Chipaya to their wives. They stayed late, as usual, reluctant to end the time of fellowship in a warm house. When they finally left, Ron slowly climbed the ladder to our sleeping loft, let the pressure out of the kerosene lamp, and crawled into bed as it flickered out. He wondered why the altitude was affecting him so much this time.

The next morning he felt worse. Then he noticed his urine was dark. Oh, no! Hepatitis! The whites of his eyes were yellow, too. No wonder he felt so tired. If the Chipayas noticed his yellow eyes, they would think the curse was taking effect and he was going blind. And what would the believers think? Would it undermine their faith? Ron was sure he'd caught hepatitis from the sick man he had treated, but they didn't understand how germs carried sickness. On our next radio schedule, he said, "I have all the symptoms of hepatitis. Please send a plane to get us."

The pilots said, "We'll come as soon as we can but our flight schedule is full for six days."

Those were six long days for Ron. He lay on the hard adobe bench in our front room, dragging himself to the door when anyone knocked. He kept his eyes averted, and as soon as the visitors left he'd drop down on the bench again. We just told folks, "The plane is coming sooner than expected," and prayed for a dry airstrip in the middle of rainy season. We told the believers, "Just stand firm in the Lord. We'll pray for you every day and return as soon as possible." We had only been in Chipaya seven weeks. We never dreamed we'd be gone for over a year and a half!

The JAARS pilots questioned the safety of flying to Chipaya again and taking off with a load, but in spite of his harrowing experience the year before, Bill Key was willing to risk it. The airstrip close to town was flooded on one end, and there was no way Ron could make it all the way to the salt-flat airstrip. This time the pilot would have to shuttle us from the close landing strip to the longer salt flat, then take off from there with all of us. First he took Ron, Debbie and Carla, then came back for Barbie and me and a bundle of diapers. With the Everlasting Arms lifting the plane, we made it.

Later, when someone asked Bill, "How was the flight?" He answered, "Well, this time I had *four* lift-offs to worry about instead of one!"

An Early Furlough
Doctors' Visits

We kept hoping Ron would recover quickly, but he didn't.

Meanwhile, Carla stumbled a lot and limped when she walked, so we checked with a pediatrician and X-rays showed her left leg wasn't in its socket. Apparently it never had been, but the doctors hadn't noticed when she was born. We decided to take her to the U.S. for treatment.

But where should we go? And where could we live? My parents were in Guatemala and Ron's folks lived in a small town which might not have skilled medical care. We wrote to friends in the U.S. for suggestions and advice. In April a nurse friend contacted the director of the Shriners' Hospital in Chicago who offered to sponsor Carla's treatment since we were missionaries with a very low income. A few days later we heard about a Christian doctor in Evanston who rented an apartment to missionaries for seventy-five dollars a month. When we heard it was available, we bought tickets to Chicago.

Carla was treated at the Shriners' Hospital and ended up wearing a cast for eleven months. Meanwhile we discovered that Debbie needed major kidney surgery. Because her condition was rather unusual, she was treated at the Illinois Research Hospital, which covered all expenses. We were so thankful!

By December Ron was finally feeling better.

News from a Far Country

We wrote to Chipaya, but heard nothing. Chipaya felt far away.

Then in January we got a letter from Maximo saying, "There are more new believers... This year there was an epidemic and cough. One hundred thirty people died. When my baby girl died, the townspeople didn't want me to bury her in the cemetery, but they finally let me. We suffered a lot..." Suddenly Chipaya felt very close, and we longed to get back.

Carla's cast came off in June, but her doctors said, "We need to check her hip at the end of summer."

Now what?

A Concordance of Chipaya Suffixes

As always, God's timing was perfect. We contacted SIL where we had first studied linguistics at Oklahoma University. They said there was still room for us in the dorm and Ron wasn't needed on staff so he could work on Chipaya language materials.

That summer Ron spent his days and evenings typing all our Chipaya texts on to IBM punch cards, hyphenating all the prefixes and suffixes. At the end of the summer the program gave us an alphabetized computer print-out of every word and suffix, showing the context of every occurrence. The delay in returning to Bolivia actually saved Ron untold hours of hand-written paperwork in analyzing the Chipaya grammar.

Finally, in September, 1965, having spent sixteen months in the U.S., everybody was given a clean bill of health. After a quick goodbye to family and friends, we headed back to Bolivia.

4
Rejection and Persecution
1965-1968

Back in Bolivia

The week we landed in Cochabamba, Ron ordered a Yamaha 80 trail model motorcycle, knowing that after his bout with hepatitis he couldn't peddle a bicycle in the altitude like he used to. The next Saturday he headed for Chipaya. His ten-and-a-half-hour trip from Oruro convinced him a motorcycle was handy for short runs but was not the answer to our transportation needs.

After greeting the Chipayas, Ron came back for the rest of us and we hired a truck to take us and our supplies. As usual, the girls and I rode in the cab, while Ron rode in the open back on top of baggage and grain bags with the other passengers. Because of early rains and getting stuck in mud holes, we almost turned back. When night fell we were in the middle of nowhere with no headlights! We drove a couple hours by the light of one directional signal until Ron helped connect one headlight to the directional light terminal. After that he squeezed into the cab to help hold the girls so they could sleep. We reached the school director's house in Escara at two in the morning, where we sort of slept until someone woke Ron at six o'clock to see a sick man. As we drove on to Chipaya we reminded the girls of the sand pile behind our house so as soon as we reached Chipaya they jumped out of the truck and ran to play in the sand.

Ron was anxious to start language work, but first we needed to make some home improvements. For days we shoveled out dirt as they cut holes in the adobe walls to put rafters for an upstairs over our front room, like we had over the kitchen. Now the girls had room to play upstairs when it was too cold or windy to be outside.

We added another window upstairs and stapled more heavy plastic to the roof poles for a ceiling.

We replaced the adobe kitchen counter with wooden shelves and a bright red linoleum counter top and added bricks which made our floor much warmer and drier than the flagstone. As soon as possible we added more straw to our leaky roof and by mid-December we had a new outhouse.

We were settling in for the long haul.

In the next seven months Ron wanted to learn to speak well, finish analyzing the grammar, start translating and write primers to teach reading.

We knew it would take lots of hard work and helpful Chipayas.

The Epidemic

As Maximo had written, a whooping cough epidemic had swept across the *altiplano* while we were in the U.S. Catholic nurses from Huachacalla had vaccinated a sick lady and a sick little girl, but unfortunately both of them died that night so the next day no one would let their children be vaccinated. The nurses finally took their vaccine to neighboring Aymara villages.

As children started dying, the Chipayas noticed that the believers' families were spared. Then they accused the believers of asking God to send this epidemic and they vowed, "When we're drunk on All Saints' Day we'll beat up all of you." But Padre Amado, the Catholic priest, arrived just then and forbade them to drink or ring the bells, as was their custom, so they had to drink secretly and couldn't form a mob to carry out their plans.

About that time, Maximo's baby girl died. When he started to bury her, the authorities said, "You can't bury her in the cemetery. It would be like burying a dog!" but they finally let him bury her in the farthest corner.

Soon after this, a hard freeze ruined part of their quinoa crop. Then some authorities said, "Maybe God is punishing us for the way we're treating the believers. We'd better stop." Some leaders even said, "We wish Ronaldo would return and pray for us."

In a town of barely nine hundred people, one hundred thirty children and five women died. It basically wiped out the babies under two years of age but Maximo's little girl was the only one who died among the believers' families, though some were very sick. Being ostracized by the community kept them from getting infected.

Glad News

The day we arrived in Chipaya, the believers met at our house from about eight at night till midnight. When we left, there had been thirteen believers. Now there were thirty-three! We were thrilled to meet the new believers and worship with them. Two interested women were also present. Their husbands, one of whom was a shaman, were out of town. Agustin chose the songs and explained them to the women in Chipaya, though sometimes his translation was purely coincidental. At times the women who couldn't read sang a falsetto descant. Ceferino read and explained a Scripture portion, while Eugene asked for testimonies. They all prayed at the same time, but in low voices. We were glad to see everyone taking part in the worship.

Then Gregoria told her story. She said, "I used to get very drunk at the fiestas and I slept with many different men. Their wives hated me and I was so miserable! Finally after one fiesta, the judge locked me up and fined me. Since I had no money, he said whoever paid my fine could have me for his wife. After Agustin paid my fine, the believers told me, 'God loves you, and Jesus forgave a woman just like you.' When I saw how they lived well, I decided to leave the old ways and enter God's Way. Now my life is very different and I have peace and joy in my heart." The visiting women knew her well and listened intently.

Chipaya Preachers

The Sunday meetings usually started late in the morning and lasted about three hours. Having Ceferino and Zenobio take turns didn't work very well and before long they just called on Ron to give the message. But if he did that, who would take the leadership when we were away? Ron suggested they take turns studying through the Gospel of Mark. Each Sunday they'd appoint someone to teach the following Sunday, and during the week that person would study with Ron.

Before long it was Agustin's turn. The Scripture was the end of chapter 1 and the beginning of chapter 2 of Mark. Tuesday evening Agustin came and read over the stories with Ron from the simplified Spanish New Testament: Jesus went out to pray then the disciples went out to look. "Look for what?" Agustin asked. He thought Jesus told the man with leprosy, "If you want to you can get well." In the story of the paralytic he thought there were four sick men; then since they couldn't see Jesus, he thought they were pulling the sick man back up through the roof. And so it went for an hour. It seemed hopeless, and we wondered what new teaching he'd have by Sunday! Fortunately he hadn't waited till Saturday night to start preparing.

Agustin came again on Thursday, Friday and Saturday nights, and also studied at home, so by Sunday he gave a very good message. He wanted the whole service in Chipaya, including all the hymns that had been translated, to be sure everyone could understand. They read from the Spanish Bible, of course, but everything else was in Chipaya.

If we had ever wondered whether they needed the Bible in their own language, those doubts were forever banished!

Strange Doctrines

There were thirty-three believers, but Ceferino and Zenobio clashed. Ceferino had not been a faithful leader, and some visiting preachers from Chile told Zenobio, "If you join *our* group, you can be the pastor of *your own* church."

One Sunday when Zenobio led the meeting, he sang a lot of unfamiliar songs, and after each one he exclaimed, "Gloria a Dios!" (Glory to God) to scare away the demons. He said, "That's our custom now."

Ron asked, "Are you going to start another church? Is Christ divided? What will the community think?" Everyone agreed it would be better to have just one Christian church.

The group from Chile taught that a small whirlwind of dust was really Satan or a demon, and should be reprimanded. During the meeting, when one whirled by outside, Zenobio jumped up and shouted out the door, "There's power in the blood of Jesus!" As it whirled away, he turned around, looking pleased, saying, "I chased the demon away."

Zenobio said, "The leaders from Chile said I should go to Chile to be converted again because my conversion in Chipaya didn't count. They also said, 'If we have faith, God *has* to give us what we ask for – and especially if we fast or climb a mountain or punish ourselves in some way.'" Eugene said, "Then I'm believing in vain because I'm still not well." Ron talked to him a long time about the apostle Paul and Timothy being sick and about Job's sufferings.

Unfortunately, Zenobio's group used only the ancient Spanish version of the Bible which they couldn't understand well, and their Bible study program consisted of reading five verses a week from the Old Testament regardless of the content or context.

A glimpse of Chipaya from the bell tower.

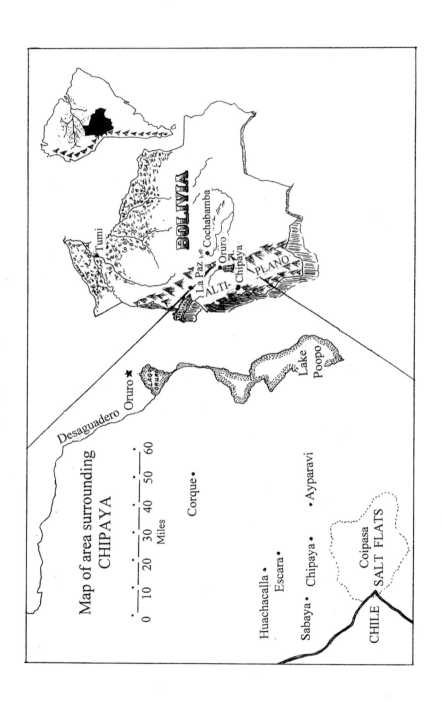

Map of area surrounding CHIPAYA

0 10 20 30 40 50 60
Miles

Desaguadero Oruro ★

LAGO CORUM

Lake Poopo

Corque •

Huachacalla •
Escara •
Sabaya • Chipaya •
Ayparavi •

Coipasa

CHILE SALT FLATS

BOLIVIA

Tumi

Cochabamba

La Paz • Oruro •
Chipaya •

ALTI- PLANO

The Bolivian "altiplano", high plane, lies between ranges of the Andes Mountains.

Llamas at a water hole.

Aerial view of the Chipaya village.

Crossing the Lauca River was always a challenge.

Sometimes even the "road" gave way.

*Our mission plane made an emergency flight
when Ron had hepatitis.*

The bell tower, visible for miles, had no church by it in 1961.

The roofs of round town houses were tied down
with a net of straw rope.

Country homes were conical, made entirely of sod blocks.

Bits of straw and little sticks helped ignite the llama dung in the three-burner mud stove.

Our house is on the right, with the diaper clothes line tied to the antenna pole.

In February, 1963, water flooded the plane as far as we could see.

*Our adobe kitchen counter held a kerosene camp stove,
box oven, and a few utensils.*

*A few years later we modernized and even had dish washers –
Debbie and Barbie!*

Ron was mechanic, "doctor", typist, photographer and taxi driver, besides linguist and Bible translator.

A Trail model Yamaha 80 became our family vehicle.

*Our girls watched Chipaya women spin and weave.
Years later they each wove a small belt.*

*Ron took our four daughters plus a visiting friend
to the river for a picnic.*

When Maxine came to wash clothes she brought her baby girl and sometimes a nursing lamb.

Children liked to wash their hands in the warm soapy water.

In a Chipaya Beauty Shop, one ancient hair style served for all.

The quinoa plant has broad leaves. It belongs to the amaranth family.

When planting quinoa, Chipayas poke a hole with a dibble stick and drop in a few grains.

After toasting the quinoa, women thresh it in a stone mortar with their bare feet serving as the pestle.

Boys dressed like their fathers and girls like their mothers.

Aurelio, like other children, helped keep the sheep and llamas from eating the quinoa.

*Bands played drums, panpipes and/or flutes for
at least 24 hours for each fiesta.*

*Tomas, never content with normal trappings,
carried three panpipes!*

Several blood-stained altars stood in front of the god houses.

Graves are above ground because the water level is so near the surface.

Barbie liked to lead blind Grandpa Sunday home.

Grandma Mary 'entered God's Way' three days before she died.

Grandpa Monday and Amy were special friends.

Two mayors hold their sacred staffs to bless the digging of an irrigation channel.

For most of eight years Ron was forced to work alone.

*Later, Maximo and others were free to help Ron
learn the language and translate.*

To speed up the translation, Ron worked in Cochabamba with Florencio.

Ron and Feliciano checked the New Testament manuscript in Chipaya.

Ceferino, the first Christian, with his wife and two daughters.

*School children liked to read Chipaya books
at our house during recess.*

*Women, who couldn't read well, sang hymns
with the help of a cassette player.*

*Our daughters and a visiting friend accompanied
the songs one Christmas.*

Easter Sunday, 1978, was Dedication Day for the Chipaya New Testament!

Men reading together from their New Testaments.

For a while the believers met in our house but then Ceferino and Zenobio met separately, each with some of the believers. Zenobio bragged, "We're closer to God and my church is stronger than Ceferino's." The community was confused.

Maximo refused to take sides, saying, "I'm just going to worship God at home."

Three Churches

Meanwhile the Catholic priests appointed Santiago to conduct Mass. He did so, but with very little training. Since all the Chipayas liked the songs, and Santiago didn't know them, he begged Maximo, "Please come teach us the songs since you're just sitting at home anyway." Maximo said, "But I'm not Catholic." Santiago insisted, "That doesn't matter. Just come teach us the songs," until finally Maximo agreed. After singing for a while, when they read from the Spanish Bible, Santiago said, "I don't understand it. What does it mean?" So Maximo explained it, and that set the pattern for the Catholic Mass.

In the end there were three churches: Zenobio's, Ceferino's and the nominal Catholic Church. The leadership usually followed the cultural pattern of one main leader plus two others of almost equal importance. As the *Middle People*, we divided our time among them, encouraging all of them to follow the Bible teachings and be true to the Lord.

Mr. President!

We had barely gotten settled after furlough when we were swamped with visitors for several weeks – including Bolivian President Barrientos who was campaigning for reelection. When he arrived, he put his arm around Ron and had Lieutenant Salomon take a picture of them. After the school children marched, the speeches began. At the end of the program the Chipayas gave the President a typical homespun outfit, minus the white felted hat. Ron had just cleaned his, so he gave it to the President, along with a copy of the Alphabet Book, Aesop's Fables, and the Easter Story. Later, Zenobio told Ron, "What you did was good! The community appreciated your giving the President your hat and they know he couldn't have come without your giving directions to the pilot by radio."

Other visitors included missionaries, national pastors, and surveyors from the International Geodesic Services. For a couple nights, we had a Ladies' Dorm and a Men's Dorm upstairs.

Another day we heard a car motor over the howling wind. Ron braved the sandstorm to meet a young British couple who was as surprised to see us as we were to see them. They were even more surprised to smell cinnamon rolls and a freshly baked apple pie!

They said, "We're in a graduate program from the University of Leeds, studying the land reform." The previous night they had slept in their new Land Rover parked crossways to the wind. By morning the paint on the ridges of their vehicle had been sand-blasted off!

Ron put 400 miles on his trusty Yamaha that first month in the village, checking on the airstrips, making a trip to Oruro, running errands to Escara, and visiting the sick.

The girls loved riding the motorcycle so Ron put a wooden seat from the handle bars to his seat for Debbie and Carla to sit on, and I'd ride behind him with Barbie on my knee. When we needed a break we'd all climb on and take a spin!

An Old Woman and a Young Man

One day an old, old woman, bent in half and leaning on a cane, hobbled up to our house and slumped down in our doorway, asking for food and coca leaves to chew. Her tousled gray braids hung limp over her ragged homespun dress.

Several young men were standing around chatting with Ron. One just laughed and said, "She's always begging for food. Her children are all away from town with their flocks." Then he laughed again. I was so angry I wished I had words to say, "Maybe someday you'll be in her place, then who will be laughing?" I got her some bread and cornmeal, and kneeled down beside her, wishing I had words to tell her of God's love. She ate a bit of the bread then struggled to her feet and hobbled away, stopping every little while to sit or lie down to rest in the shade of a house or doorway. My heart ached as I watched her. Why were people so cruel?

The next morning that same fellow was in terrible pain, probably from kidney stones, so Ron gave him strong pain medication. I said, "Maybe that's his punishment for being so hard-hearted." Ron said, "Don't suggest it or he'll think we cursed him, and no telling what he'd do to get even!" The man must have recovered quickly because by afternoon he was out dancing at the fiesta.

Studying Alone

The Chipayas were angry with the believers for not helping placate the spirits, and angry with us for stealing their language. The unbelievers wanted us out of the picture saying, "If Olson is gone, the believers will fall, then they'll all help with the rituals and sacrifices again." Maximo said, "No way." When Ron talked to one or two fellows alone, they sometimes helped him with a word or two, but if others were around, there was stony silence.

When the Bolivian school year ended in November, Ron got permission to study in the new school which was nice and light – with glass windows! He even had room on the desk for his books and the big concordance from SIL. It was worth its weight in gold now, showing the context of every suffix, as he tried to figure out the grammar rules. He said, "It's like a huge jigsaw puzzle with thousands of pieces!" He was seldom interrupted because no one wanted to be accused of teaching him the language. The believers desperately needed the Scriptures, but he couldn't translate until he understood the grammar better.

September, October, and November slipped by with almost no language help. In December when Ceferino went to Oruro, we sent letters to family and friends begging them to pray that people would help us learn the language.

Then December and January slipped by. Ron felt drained by the late nights with visitors and believers, long motorcycle trips in the altitude, the church problems and working so hard by himself on the grammar. His goals looked unreachable. At times he was so tired and discouraged he wondered if he'd last until April.

Language Help at Last!

Then slowly, in February, folks started answering his questions about the language. Inexplicably the mayor himself, who had been strongly opposed to our language work, offered to help Ron, and actually encouraged others to do so. Now the men talked freely to him, giving him conversational practice, and even working with him openly in the school. We could hardly believe it! The whole atmosphere had changed.

What made the difference? Was it the prayers of folks who received our Christmas letter? Or was it the strong words from Dr. Lopez of UNESCO telling the authorities to cooperate with us? Whatever the reason, we said "Thank you, Lord!" In a few weeks Ron understood the grammar enough to start translating.

For all of March Ron had as much language help as he could use. It was wonderful! Maximo was an excellent helper in translating the Gospel of Mark as they pondered how to translate words like "baptize" and "repent." Some expressions had to be adjusted:

"The time is fulfilled" became "This time is tired"

"Believe the Gospel" – "Buy God's saving Word"

"A man with an unclean spirit" – "A man grabbed by a demon"

"They were all amazed" – "The people lost their heart"

"Heads of grain" – "Noses of wheat"

"House of God" – "Church-house of God" (because their "house of God" was a little box holding an idol)

"Sons of Thunder" – "Very out-spoken, or strong-speaking, like thunder" (because "sons of thunder" would be understood as "sons of the devil")

Besides translating Mark, Ron worked on the Christmas story, stories from Genesis, songs, and transitional readers to teach Spanish readers to read Chipaya. Miraculously, by April Ron had reached his ambitious goals.

A Grammar Lesson

A businessman from La Paz visited Chipaya one time. He said, "I'd like to know everything about the Chipayas because I might be distantly related to them. I'd like to learn their language." Ron said, "Okay," so after lunch the gentleman came for a Chipaya grammar lesson. Opening his notebook, he said, "I'll take notes while you explain it to me, so I can learn to speak it. It's probably not very complicated since the people aren't so civilized."

Ron suggested, "Let's start with an example: 'The man fed the baby quinoa.'

The indirect object, *Wawqui* (baby), comes first;

then the direct object, *cula* (quinoa);

then the verb, *lujl-kat-ni-chi-zakaz-qui-chicha.*

The subject is implicit in the verb:

-*lujl* – to eat;

-*kat* – caused to;

-*ni* – habitually;

-*chi* – he;

-*zakaz* – also;

-*qui* – so they say, but I didn't see him do it;

-*chicha* – this makes it all a verb."

"That one word says all that?"

"Oh, yes, but that's not all. Other suffixes can tell you where he did it, if he has finished doing it, how he did it or if he should have done it, or if he intends to do it, etc., but the suffixes have to come in the right order. The same syllable can mean different things, depending where it comes in the line-up." After an hour of grammatical explanations our visitor closed his notebook saying, "Well, I probably wouldn't use it much anyway." Standing up to leave he said, "Thank you. I'll be back in a little while for tea."

The Cure for a Curse

Maximo's sister, Sabina, had been interested in the Gospel for a long time, but her husband's family was deeply involved in rituals and witchcraft. When her husband, Albino, became very sick, the shaman said, "Your own father has cursed you." Albino finally recovered, but then their baby boy got sick. The shaman said, "The curse has passed on to your baby." Several other shamans agreed, but one added, "It's true. Your father's curse has passed on to your baby and he *will* die – unless you become a believer!" (This shaman had previously been interested in following God, but when he got married his in-laws violently opposed the Gospel and turned him back to the old ways.) As Albino considered the Gospel, the more he thought about the demons, saints, rituals and fiestas, the more fed up be became. Finally after Carnival, he and Sabina joined the believers. At the same time they asked, "Can children also enter God's Way? Our son, Roberto says he wants to. He's twelve years old." Ron said, "Of course he can!"

Previously, their family had to avoid many places which were taboo to them. Now they walked freely wherever they chose and with prayer and medicine, their baby boy was soon lively and well. They had lost all their other children except Roberto, so little David was precious to them.

A few days later Albino asked Ron, "Would you go with me to destroy my old shrine?" Ron said, "Whenever you say." So one afternoon Albino led the way on his bicycle while Ron and I, with our three little girls, followed on the motorcycle. We waded across the first icy river, carrying the girls, but when we reached the second river I was a coward. It was about thirty feet wide, almost knee deep, with chunks of ice floating in it. In some shallow places it was still frozen half way across. Albino carried his bicycle across while Ron parked the motorcycle and walked the rest of the way.

I watched the girls play while Ron and Albino leveled the shrine and scattered the debris. No more animals would be sacrificed to *that* spirit!

Time Out in the Jungle and the City

Amazingly, when it was time to leave for conference, the ground was dry enough and the river low enough that all five of us could ride the motorcycle to Escara and catch a truck to Oruro. By the time we reached Tumi Chucua, our mission center in the jungle, we had traveled by motorcycle, foot, truck, barge, taxi, train, Jeep, commercial plane and the small JAARS plane.

After conference we flew to Cochabamba. Instead of one long reading book we decided to print five short readers, each with a certificate at the end, plus two correlated story books. By the end of November they were printed. The story of Aurelio's Christmas had just been printed in a Sunday school paper in the States so we were counting on many people praying for the Chipayas. We looked forward to busy, happy days in the village, translating a lot – never dreaming of the heartache that awaited us.

Before returning to Chipaya, Ron checked on the promised school supplies and the CARE foods, since the two previous quinoa crops hadn't been enough to feed their families. The truck we hired to take the CARE food to Chipaya was so large we all fit in the cab. That was our best and quickest trip ever, arriving by five in the evening but then the altitude hit me and I gave out. Ron fixed supper, cared for the girls, tended to the visitors and talked to the food supervisor. He felt the altitude, too, but said, "Just old age creeping up." We spent the first week distributing food according to the mayors' lists of families. Unfortunately, the free-food program seemed to generate more greed and ill will than appreciation.

We were thankful our girls played so well with each other and our neighbors, Ismael and his little brothers. They were learning a bit of Spanish together, since our girls spoke English and the boys spoke Aymara.

Daniel Condori

One Monday some men told Ron, "Daniel Condori is very sick. Please go see him in Escara." Ron took some strong antibiotics and hopped on his motorcycle. It was too true. Daniel could hardly breathe and was so weak he couldn't cough. Apparently he was in the last stages of tuberculosis. His mouth was foamy and he couldn't speak clearly. For a long time he had been interested in the Gospel but had never entered God's Way because his wife was so opposed. Now he knew it was his last chance, so when Ron asked him if he wanted to enter God's Way, he said, "Yes," and prayed, "God, please forgive my sins and save me." Ron gave him antibiotics, left more with the family, and came home, wondering if he would live through the night.

Tuesday they called Ron again, saying, "He's still alive and they're bringing him home because he doesn't want to die in Escara." Ron rode out to meet him. They had already been on the road over four hours, carrying Daniel on a couple cactus planks suspended between two bicycles! Though very weak, he could speak clearly and wasn't foaming but the trip was too much for him and about an hour after Ron met them, he died. His wife had gone on ahead, so she didn't know he had died till they reached home.

My heart ached for Benigna, his widow. I didn't know her well, but the first year we were in Chipaya she had sold me the Chipaya dress I was wearing.

But It's Supper Time!

The next day someone knocked on my kitchen door – right at supper time. All day I'd been carrying water from the well, scrubbing clothes, fixing meals and taking care of my three little girls, plus straining to understand the words when Chipayas came to our door, and groping for words to answer them.

By sundown I was exhausted. Maybe if I ignored whoever was knocking they'd go away.

But no. They knocked again. I wished they would at least go to the front door and talk to Ron. Why did they have to come to the kitchen – my only place of retreat in the whole village?

When they knocked the third time, I sighed and opened the door, just a little. I didn't recognize the woman. They all looked alike in their dark homespun dresses and long black braids. "Hello, sister, I've come to visit," she said, fingering my sweater, so soft, compared to her rough homespun dress. From the doorway, she stared past me at my kitchen which seemed so luxurious to her – plastic tablecloth, curtains on the windows, dishes and pans on apple-crate shelves. Running her grimy fingers over the closest Tupperware canister she asked, "What's this? What's in it? Can I taste it? Please give me some!"

Impatiently I said, "Sister, I don't have time to visit now. My children are hungry, and I have to cook supper for my husband." Then her head drooped and her tone changed. "Oh, little sister," she wailed softly, "I'm all alone. My husband died! What am I going to do? What are my children going to do?"

Then I realized she was Benigna, whose husband had been buried in the little cemetery that very afternoon. Again she wailed, "Oh, little sister, he died! He's gone! Now I'm all alone. He was so sick... Ohhhhhh!" Her lonely, hopeless wail was worse than anything I had ever heard.

Gently I drew her into my kitchen and shut the door. I put my arm around her and tried to speak but no words came. Only tears. I found we cried in the same language.

Slowly I regained composure, remembering that her husband had prayed to God before dying. Through my own tears I tried to comfort her. "Your husband is not dead. He is not even sick. He entered God's Way. Now he is in heaven with God. If you enter God's Way, too, God will care for you and your children. And you'll see your husband again when you go to God's town in heaven." I didn't know I could say those things in her language. It almost seemed like someone else was speaking through me.

Slowly she wiped her eyes and cheeks with the back of her hand. In a few minutes no one could have guessed she had been crying. Squeezing my hand, she whispered, "Thank you, sister!" then turned and hurried out into the night.

Supper, somehow, didn't seem so all-important any more.

That weekend, after talking to Gregoria and the other believers, Benigna entered God's Way. It was the first time I had had a part in a Chipaya woman becoming a child of God – and to think I almost missed it because it was *supper time*!

Now she loves to sit on our brick floor and sing with me. Her favorite song is the stanza of "Jesus Loves Me" which says, "He never leaves me alone. Christ is with me, so I'm not afraid of anything." Since she can't read, we sing it over and over till it sinks into her heart – even if it gets to be supper time.

Crime and Punishment

After distributing the CARE food, Ron was finally free to resume translating the Gospel of Mark with Maximo. Everything was moving along nicely then – on December 22, Eulogio was caught in adultery! Eulogio, one of the first believers. Eulogio, whose beautiful, girlish wife Petrona had borne him two little boys. Eulogio, the first honest person we had ever met in Chipaya. We didn't want to believe it, but there was no denying it. Our hearts ached for Petrona, for him, and for what it would do to the testimony of Jesus.

They dragged Eulogio to the judge on Friday. A large, curious crowd quickly gathered at the *courthouse* behind our house.

"Why have you brought him? What's he done?" the judge demanded.

"He committed adultery. We caught him in the very act."

"And a few months ago he tried to rape a girl."

"And it isn't the first time. He has committed adultery with two or three others."

"It's more times than that. At least five or six times. It's his habit."

"Bring his Bible and songbook and any other Christian tracts or papers he has in his house," the judge demanded. "And make his family bring money to buy coca and alcohol and cigarettes for everybody present!"

The accusations and ravings increased as they all drank and smoked and chewed coca leaves hour after hour. Their smoldering anger against the believers for leaving the old ways and not sharing the burden of pacifying all their spirit gods, was fanned into flames, all focused on Eulogio. The judge kept the case going far into the night, contrary to Bolivian law. Justice went by the board. Accusations kept growing.

"The other believers probably do the same thing."

"They probably teach their followers to do that."

"I'm sure they do! They are all adulterers."

"That's what they do when they get together."

Then the judge commanded, "Tie him up! Beat him!" They tied his arms and ankles, and made him kneel on the floor, and then they whipped, kicked and beat him, at times with his own Bible, demanding, "Admit it! That's what your church teaches, isn't it? We know it's true and we won't quit beating you till you admit it!"

Finally he said, "Yes, yes, it's true."

Then they said, "We're going to force you to become an unbeliever and be responsible for rituals and sacrifices. We're going to make all the believers take part in sacrifices and rituals for the fiestas. We're going to stamp out evangelical Christianity in Chipaya! Promise you'll quit being an evangelical or we won't stop beating you!"

Finally, when he didn't think he could take any more, he said, "Yes, I'll quit. I'll quit," and he slumped on the floor.

The beating and threats frightened the believers and others who were interested in becoming believers. They said, "If they're going to beat us and force us to do rituals, what can we do? Maybe we'd better return to the old ways." Ron used the opportunity to teach what the Bible says about persecution, denying the Lord, what our Lord suffered, etc. Things looked dark.

Some unbelievers said, "If this is the Gospel and Eulogio is a believer, I don't want it." Others who had been interested in the Gospel said, "What's the use of it if the leaders are sick and commit adultery?" Of the six early believers, Maximo and Eugenio were sick, Ceferino was gone most of the time, Zenobio and Agustin were splitting the church, and now Eulogio was caught in adultery.

Zenobio made things worse by saying, "Yes, Ceferino's church teaches adultery. Probably many are adulterers. They are simple and weak. But my Gospel is strong. Join my group!" He promised Eulogio, "I'll help you in court if you join my group," so Eulogio said, "Okay."

The next night, which was Christmas Eve, it froze – something very unusual for the middle of summer. Christmas night it froze even harder, damaging the quinoa crop. It was as though the Lord stepped in and said, "Enough!" The community became alarmed. "Our quinoa crop will be ruined! Why did the judge tie up Eulogio and beat him?" they demanded. "Why are the authorities mistreating all the believers? Now God is going to destroy our whole crop and the authorities are to blame!"

A few days later, when Eulogio's case came up in court, the whole atmosphere had changed. There were no claims against the other believers; no word against the Bible, God, or the church, and Eulogio's Bible was returned to him.

We were thankful the community had calmed down but the problem of weak believers, no spiritual leader, and Zenobio's divisive ways still remained.

On Monday, dear, faithful Pastor Napoleon bicycled into town, just when the believers needed him most. He told Zenobio, "All the Christians in La Paz are united, and you need to be united in Chipaya. If you can help the church be united, maybe you can take part in the leadership."

In the midst of all this turmoil, four single young men, relatives of believers, said they wanted to become Christians. Alejandro and his wife said, "We want to follow God and join Zenobio's group." Ron said, "That's great! But church names and people's names can't save you. Only Jesus Christ saves you." That evening they entered God's Way, but as soon as Ron left the meeting, Zenobio said, "Only my group is strong and close to God and our customs are most important."

Wednesday, when all the believers except Zenobio met again, they decided to scratch Eulogio's name from the church list because of his denial. After Pastor Napoleon read and discussed verses about love, divisions and names, they all agreed to stay united.

As soon as Napoleon left town, however, Zenobio announced, "Napoleon said there should be only one church in Chipaya and I should be its leader." He told the new believers, "You should go with me to a special church in another town to accept the Lord because your conversion in Chipaya isn't valid."

No matter how disappointed or aggravated we felt toward Zenobio, however, we realized he wasn't the enemy: Satan was the one trying to destroy the Christian church. The last week of 1966 was truly a dark, heavy time.

Other Chipayas were interested in the Good News of the Gospel but didn't admit it openly for fear of the community. Alexander bought a Bible, but on his wedding day one of his in-laws confiscated it saying, "No relative of mine is going to be an evangelical!" We didn't see him after that. When another man built a little chapel near his country home to worship God, his neighbors used it as a toilet. He finally gave up and returned to the old ways.

Folks slowly settled down so that by the last Sunday of January twenty-six people from eight families came to church. By then, Zenobio and Agustin had their own church and were trying to get us thrown out of Chipaya.

Justice? In Chipaya

During Mardi Gras, the Chipaya authorities told the believers, "Since you don't take part in the fiesta anyway, you're appointed to keep the animals away from the quinoa plants. If necessary, pen them up in the corrals."

After the fiesta a believer reported one pig was in a corral, but late one night, ten days later, a drunk official summoned the believer and charged him with the death of the pig. The wrangling lasted almost till morning. In spite of the fact that the believer had reported the pig was locked up, he was judged guilty and fined for the pig and for ignoring the first order to appear in court late at night. Such was justice in Chipaya.

Yesterday, Today and Tomorrow

Yesterday their big dark eyes were smiling. Just two little sisters in dark, homespun dresses with neat rows of tiny braids. They stood in our open doorway, quietly stepping aside to let others in or out. Their mother, Modesta, had left the flocks and walked to town for a community work day, to build a new school. Children were to stay out of the way.

For several hours the little girls stood by our door as I sat at the desk writing Bible stories to be translated into their language. About noon I read them the booklet that summarized the life of Jesus, the first Bible story book in their language. I pointed to the pictures on each page, lingering on the page of Jesus with the children. They seemed to understand, and smiled shyly. I was surprised when Victoria, the older one, whispered an answer to a question. For years her ears had been draining and her mother said she was deaf. I asked if their mom and dad listened to God's Word. Little Antoca said, "Mother does, and sometimes Father does, but he's working far away in another town. He's been gone a long time. That's why Mother is carrying adobes."

Later in the day Victoria whispered, "I'd like a doll." On other visits to the village I had spent most of my time helping ladies and children sew rag dolls, but this time I didn't have cloth or time. I wished I could make her one, but if I managed to find scraps (and time) for just one doll, how would other little girls feel? It was so hard to say No, but what else could I do?

Later in the evening their mother came for medicine. She was pleased that I remembered her. How could I forget? She was Modesta, one of my first friends who five years earlier had braided my short brown hair into seventy-seven tiny braids like theirs. For years she had avoided us, not caring to hear about a *new* God, but recently she had begun to listen to God's Word. She seemed pleased that her little girls had spent most of the day at our house.

That was yesterday. They were all smiling.

But today was different.

I didn't sense it when they first came and stood watching me.

I thought maybe they were still hoping for a little rag doll. I was checking the Bible stories, and didn't notice when they slipped away.

About noon I noticed a crowd by the *courthouse* and realized their mother was on trial for adultery last night. The self-righteous accusers, the condemning authorities, the curious crowd – they were all there, just like in Jesus' day – everyone except the man involved.

I saw the little sisters for an instant in the afternoon, but their smiles had vanished, leaving a dull, empty nothingness. When I smiled at little Victoria she looked up at her mother, searching her emotionless face for permission to respond to my smile – but received nothing. Then in a moment all three were gone.

My heart ached for all of them and the tears came. In the same situation Jesus said, "Neither do I [condemn you]. Go and sin no more." (John 8:11) But she couldn't read very well and the New Testament wasn't even printed in her language yet.

I prayed, "Dear Father, tomorrow, please help her remember what she's heard from your Word – or help one of the believers go to her in love and lead her back – or bring her here again so I can read those verses to her from the typed manuscripts. Tomorrow, Lord, please bring her back into fellowship with you – so she can smile again.

And her two little girls, as well."

A Daily Struggle

Besides the other problems, a siege of mumps, flu and dysentery was going around, and Ron was the only doctor. Exhausted and discouraged, one day, he wrote:

"I've never seen so many forms of evil – evil people and evil leaders committed to evil… The powers of evil are determined to destroy the believers, to drive us out of Chipaya, and to prevent others from entering God's Way.

"The future course of Chipaya is being set. Civic leaders have considered the Gospel, turned away, and now are set against it. Evil continues to gain the upper hand in most of the Chipayas. They have no concern for justice, for Bolivian law, for reason, or for mercy. They scorn the poor and mistreat the aged and orphans. All the wickedness and immorality make me think of Sodom and Gomorrah." (Genesis 19)

But then he looked at the brighter side, and added:

"In spite of all this, God has drawn and kept some believers faithful in spite of tremendous pressures and temptations. We have had good meetings, with twenty-four or twenty-five believers attending – but it is a daily struggle."

Several individuals, including Zenobio's brother Ramon, our one-time antagonist, expressed interest in following God, but unless both husband and wife entered God's Way, neither of them did. Chipayas were so bound up in rituals and spirit worship that they couldn't live together if one was on the Wide Path and the other on God's Narrow Path. (Matt. 7:13-14) There was no middle ground. At times it was sad to see the interested one turn away, but on the other hand, coming as families made for a strong church.

Bread for Reading

Ron printed thirty songbooks, with seven hymns and six choruses, on the hectograph and stapled construction paper covers on them. Until now we had used carbon copies. The believers happily bought two song books for four cents! They liked to sing all the songs each time we met.

Sometimes on Saturday, when families came to town, I'd sit on our floor with the ladies and sing by the hour. Wanting to learn the songs, they'd try to follow along in their songbooks even though they only recognized a few letters. I was glad when Ron, Ceferino and Maximo recorded the songs so we could sing along with the cassette tapes which didn't get hoarse like I did.

Our series of five reading books were printed now and even Aurelio was delighted to find he could read the first few lessons. The school children came running to our house at recess to borrow the primers and the bright students could have learned to read Chipaya quickly but Ron said, "We need to teach the church leaders to read first. If the children learn first, the adults will back off to save face and never learn to read well. It is crucial for the church leaders to read first."

But when could they study? Most of them spent all week in their country homes. By night they were too tired to concentrate and fell asleep. By the end of church on Sunday they were hungry, and by the time they went home and cooked a meal, it was time to walk back to their country homes. Then we had an idea: since they loved our homemade bread, why not serve bread at the end of church for those who stayed for reading classes? The next Saturday I baked several loaves of bread in our little box oven and after church we invited everyone to stay and read. It worked! They loved the bread and we were delighted they were learning to read.

Women who had never been to school studied Book 1. Those who had attended school could read Book 1 and 2 which only used letters which were the same in the Spanish alphabet. The other three books taught new letters and combinations of consonants, one at a time. The men started by reading Book 2 in unison (sort of!), and going on from there.

We marked each one's progress on a big chart. By mid-February, fifteen men had finished Book 2. By the end of March six had read all five primers and four more had finished four books.

Zenobio wanted to read Chipaya, but was quite a slow learner and didn't come very often to practice. We wished he would learn, especially since he was a church leader and didn't understand the Spanish Bible very well. But in spite of not reading well he was a faithful and enthusiastic leader, visiting and encouraging new believers and sick folks. His family built a chapel and he also started a home church in the Chipaya settlement of Ayparavi using the Spanish Bible and Chipaya songbook.

Non-believers weren't interested in reading Chipaya.

Translating the Gospel of Mark

Maximo was suffering from a strange disease, and wading across the cold rivers aggravated the painful welts on both legs. Ron searched in vain through the *Merck Manual* for a diagnosis and cure. Although Maximo was sick and discouraged by Zenobio's divisive ways; he was willing to translate, so Ron rode his Yamaha to Maximo's country home to work with him.

Ceferino was the first and only Chipaya believer for over two years before we arrived. We expected him to be like a pastor to the new believers, but his heart was set on making money selling sheep cheese or woven goods. The same week that Eulogio had his moral problem, Ceferino's world also caved in. After borrowing a teacher's typewriter in Oruro, he left it in a taxi by mistake, so he owed the teacher two hundred fifty pesos. Added to a previous debt of five hundred pesos, he was now working just to pay the monthly interest of fifty pesos.

In January Ceferino told Ron, "I think I should stay in Chipaya, help the church, and work on translation with you. If you would loan me the money to pay off my debts, I could do that." Ron said, "Okay, and you can pay me back by translating." Unfortunately, the first week of January Ceferino had to go to Chile. The second and third weeks he had business in Oruro and the fourth week he had community service.

In the meantime Ron tried working with Albino, but he was poor to start with, and deteriorated till he was no help at all.

Finally in February, when Ceferino worked with Ron for the first time in five years, Ron found he was an excellent translator – even better than Maximo. In three good days, they polished nine chapters of Mark. But the next week Ceferino had to help divert the river which was flooding the quinoa fields, then he attended special meetings in another town, and had to go to Oruro again – and that shot the rest of February! When he finally showed up in March, the authorities nabbed him concerning another problem. Ron loaned him money again to pay his fine so they wouldn't confiscate his bike.

Ron tried to translate on his own but it was close to Mardi Gras and there was too much commotion day and night.

The following Monday Ceferino finally came back to work, but Tuesday he had to help divert the river again. Ron had hoped to finish Mark by March 9, but it didn't happen. Then Ceferino announced, "The community wants me to be magistrate for all of Chipaya next year. What do you think?" Ron said, "The job would take all your time and I think it would be a headache. Some people would expect more of you for being a believer, and others would oppose you for the same reason." But in spite of the drawbacks Ceferino seemed to want the prestige.

They had barely finished Mark when Ceferino said, "Worms are eating our crops. I have to harvest my quinoa immediately," – and he was gone again.

Finally, on March 25, Ron and Maximo made the final corrections on the Gospel of Mark.

Ron wrote, "In four months, we've barely translated Mark. At this rate, when would we ever finish the New Testament? It looks like we need to bring Ceferino to Cochabamba if we are going to make any progress at all. It's good to be here to teach and encourage the believers but there are too many interruptions to do much translation."

So Ron decided that in the village he would help the Chipayas in whatever way they needed – as doctor, mechanic, carpenter, typist or whatever – and concentrate on translation in the city. We were glad Maximo and Ceferino said they were willing to work in Cochabamba for a few weeks at a time.

Friendly Neighbors

Conference time was approaching again and as usual we wondered how we'd get to Oruro. Just then Sabina said, "The Aymaras captured my husband, Albino, and locked him up on false charges in Huachacalla. Please take him some food and money to pay his bail. If any of us go, they might lock us up, too." Ron said "Okay," and asked Ceferino to go along to help carry the motorcycle across the river. When they got to Huachacalla, however, Albino had already been sent to Oruro, so Ron stopped to visit Padre Amado and the other priests at their Catholic mission station before heading home. As they chatted, they realized they both had two-way radios, and decided to try to communicate with each other. It worked!

A few days later Ron met two priests at the river and gave them a ride to Chipaya on his motorcycle. At lunch they happened to mention that Padre Amado was driving to Oruro on Sunday. Ron said, "I can't leave quite yet because I'm expecting a visitor next week, but do you think Padre Amado could take my wife and little girls to Oruro?" They said, "Why not?" So Friday Ron took the girls and me on the motorcycle to the river where we waded across and boarded the priests' vehicle. The nuns put us up in their clinic in Huachacalla and the next day Padre Amado drove us to Oruro where we spent a couple nights in the convent waiting for the Tuesday train to Cochabamba. Madrecita Juanina was delighted to see Debbie after five years, and to meet Carla and Barbie! Such neat neighbors!

Ron's visitor never arrived in Chipaya so he finally rode his motorcycle out the back way to Oruro.

Our four months in Chipaya had been disappointing in view of Eulogio's moral lapse; some new believers turning back; two others spreading confusion and discord; and searching and waiting in vain many times for translation helpers.

But we were encouraged in other ways: there was one new Christian couple; most believers had remained faithful in spite of testing; the Gospel of Mark was almost ready to print; the grammar write-up was complete; ten believers had read four or five primers; and we had had no serious illness.

As we left Chipaya we never dreamed this would be our last long stay in the village.

Other Jobs

Back in Cochabamba, we packed cool clothes for Tumi Chucua. This time we would live at the jungle center while consultants checked the Gospel of Mark and our grammar write-up. As the new chairman of the Executive Committee, Ron would have more group responsibilities in the coming year.

After conference, the girls and I stayed at Tumi while Ron flew to Mexico to be trained as a translation consultant. The girls were happy for playmates of the same color and language. Debbie was in first grade now, Carla in kindergarten and Barbie in pre-school. My assignment was to draw illustrations for primers and Bible stories and help translators get booklets ready to print since I had worked in the print shop. As several folks used the same illustrations and format for their Bible stories, we flooded the print shop with book orders! My goal was also to write stories about all the main Bible characters and events from Adam and Eve to Moses and Joshua.

After returning from Mexico, Ron led a two-month workshop at Tumi to help translators solve linguistic and translation problems in their languages. He was also compiling notes from commentaries to help translators understand the Apostle Paul's letter to the Corinthian Christians. Knowing Greek was helpful for this project as well as for translating.

In mid-December our family returned to Cochabamba where Ron worked on translation and commentary compilations.

Searching for Pictures

All the translators in the different language groups wanted to publish easy-to-read booklets and Bible stories for new readers, with a picture and just a few lines of text on each page, but the problem was finding illustrations. In January, Ron translated stories about Creation, Adam and Eve, and The Flood. My job was to illustrate them. For Creation we pictured local plants, animals, etc. For the story of Adam and Eve, I dressed four-year-old Barbie in big fig leaves pinned together with little sticks! Pictures of Noah were plentiful, but the ark looked different in every one. I did my best but it was *far* from professional.

Ron wrote to many Christian organizations searching for series of pictures but found very few. Unfortunately there was no Internet in 1968! The Moody Bible Institute sent a filmstrip of "Elijah and the Prophets of Baal," and Bibla-Vision in Japan sent a set of picture cards for the Christmas story. Our printer photographed the filmstrip and cards which I retouched. It was a big job, but easier than drawing freehand. Then a translator drew pictures to illustrate the story of "The Prodigal Son." With these illustrations available, Ron translated the stories of Elijah, Christmas and the Prodigal Son. He also asked an Aymara artist for a series of line drawings to illustrate verses in 1 John.

Our long search for biblical illustrations finally ended when the David C. Cook Foundation gave us permission to use the artwork from their "Sunday PIX" weekly paper, at no cost whatsoever. We were *so* thankful! I immediately adapted pictures for five stories about Moses which were already translated.

When the Cook Foundation sent each set of black-and-white proof pages, I covered the conversation balloons and filled in the trees, houses or whatever was missing. After photographing the adapted pictures, we returned the original proof pages. It was *wonderful* to have a beautiful series of pictures for the whole Bible at our fingertips!

Short Trips to Chipaya

A few months later, as soon as The Gospel of Mark was printed, Ron and a colleague made a quick trip to Chipaya to take five Bible stories and The Gospel of Mark. They sold twenty sets of Bible stories at the bargain price of five books for one peso – eight cents! They sold a few copies of Mark, but it was difficult for the Chipayas to read a full page of text.

On Sunday Ron met with Zenobio's group, where he read from Mark and said a few words. Zenobio bought a copy of Mark and made a speech about how good it was for us to be there and how grateful he was that we brought the Gospel to Chipaya. What a change from wanting to throw us out of town! Once Zenobio got his following, he had quit talking against us and the other believers.

Eulogio had joined Zenobio's group and now Eulogio's mother and three new couples had also joined. We had opposed the church split, but now Ron said, "Maybe it will result in more believers after all." Now the Christian community numbered forty adults, almost fifteen percent of all the Chipayas. Many new believers were relatives of earlier believers.

At the same time, Pentecostal churches were springing up all across the *altiplano* because groups of Pentecostal believers frequently held conferences and special meetings in new areas.

While in Chipaya, Ron helped build a square room to house

an old-fashioned motor for electric lights, which the government had promised. The community bought fifty poles and the Prefect offered to buy the first 1,000 meters of wire plus bulbs and fixtures for the school and one light bulb for every fifty meters on the streets. Ron got the used light plant working so one evening they had lights for an hour and a quarter! Everyone was delighted. Now they could dream about having electric lights every night!

In December Ron rode his Yamaha to Chipaya again to take the Christmas story. In February, when he headed to Chipaya for the third time, the roads were flooded. However, in Oruro he found Guzman, a young believer who was happy to check 1 John and the Bible stories. They worked eight hours a day for a week; the most productive week Ron had ever had.

Associate Director

Ron had been chairman of the Executive Committee, but now the director said, "I need you to be Associate Director for linguistic and translation work. I realize it will slow down your own translation, but it will speed up the other fourteen." Ron accepted reluctantly. That meant we would live at Tumi again, since most translators worked in the lowlands but first Ron went to Mexico for further training.

When he returned, he made a quick trip to Chipaya to tell the believers he wouldn't have much time to work on translation the coming year, but encouraged them to study the books they had. Although his visits to Chipaya were short that year, he did first-draft translation whenever possible.

As Associate Director, Ron challenged all the translators to consider what they wanted to accomplish in their language groups besides translating the New Testament, and to set long-term goals for achieving those ends. All the translators thought they could meet their goals in four to sixteen years if indigenous leaders could be trained in their language groups. In response, our mission started a Leadership Training Course in December for thirty indigenous folks from eight different language groups, giving practical training to teachers, mechanics, nurses, radio men, agriculturalists and cattlemen. Unfortunately, because of distance and culture, it wasn't practical to include the Chipayas.

The following year Ron was appointed Associate Director again.

5

WELCOMED AT LAST!
1969-1977

THE TIDE TURNS

Each time we returned to Chipaya we found new believers and when Ron visited in 1969, the whole atmosphere had changed. Whereas the believers had been ridiculed outcasts, as their numbers grew and they were good neighbors, they became respected members of the community again. Even some community leaders had entered God's Way, and others were interested. Chipayas in general were also friendlier toward us.

We could hardly believe it when Feliciano left the old ways to follow Christ – the proud and arrogant Feliciano who used to lead the drunken fiesta processions carrying the head of a sacrificed ram under his arm; Feliciano who chased the believers out of town and beat them; who just last year demanded we pay an exorbitant price for the privilege of living in Chipaya. What had changed his heart? Would we get a chance to ask him? He knew Spanish well and was very aggressive. He had already read much of his Spanish New Testament, and could sing hymns by the hour. The change in him was astounding!

Benito was another new believer. He borrowed the set of reading books one evening and stayed up till he had read all of them. Before long he was teaching others to read.

Ceferino and three other believers had been chosen as authorities – with no religious strings attached! With so many believers, the burden of sacrificing to all the spirits was too heavy for the unbelievers. Then West-Side came up with a daring plan – to appoint believers to *all* the official posts for one year and stop *all* sacrifices! They went even further, saying, "Maybe we should take all the idols out of our god-house and use it for Christian worship. Those who want to keep their idols can put them in the big (Catholic) church which belongs to the whole town."

East-Side was also showing interest in the God of the Bible, but not as much as West-Side.

Maximo said, "I think many in Ayparavi will enter God's Way at the end of the ritual year after fulfilling their commitments."

Although Ceferino had built a chapel, his group was like sheep without a shepherd because he was usually away on town business or as president of Chipaya's first "Agricultural Cooperative."

The Catholic group was strongest because of Maximo's teaching. Santiago, the appointed leader, wanted to build a new church instead of meeting in the big Catholic church where unbelievers sacrificed animals to the images, but Padre Amado said "No, don't build another church and distance yourself from the community." Padre Amado also said, "It's okay to drink and dance a *little* and enjoy the fiestas. Make them Christian fiestas." But Maximo said, "It's not possible for Chipayas to drink just a little."

Meanwhile, Aymara Christians in La Paz were using their five-tone musical scale to compose hymns which spread quickly all across the *altiplano*. When Ron and Maximo translated some of them, the Chipayas loved them and learned them quickly, though the tunes were harder for *us* to learn. Maximo said, "There's little interest in reading, but singing may change that."

The new songbooks with fourteen hymns and ten choruses sold quickly, and folks listened to the tapes and sang for hours at a time.

Now more townsfolk were interested in what God had to say. Whenever Ron talked to folks about the Bible, he always read from the Spanish Bible, so they would base what they believed on what God's Word said, not on what *he* said.

In his windows of time, Ron translated Paul's letters to Timothy and the Thessalonians.

An Adventure

Ron made numerous motorcycle trips to Chipaya and I had often wanted to do it just once. October, 1969, seemed to be the right time in spite of the fact that I had just become pregnant. A friend said, "A healthy apple is hard to shake," and I trusted I was carrying a healthy apple! Warm clothes, lunch, water and gas was all we could carry so we sent Bible stories, hymnbooks and Spanish New Testaments and Bibles with a fellow traveler. Barbie was going with us, too, because as a first grader she was too young to stay in the children's home. She was glad her school books were too heavy to take along.

It was a cold morning as we set off from Oruro across the *altiplano* on the Yamaha 80 with Barbie sandwiched between Ron and me. The first few hours we made good time as the infamous mud flats were hard and smooth. Then we hit sand. As the sun rose higher, we stopped to shed another jacket or sweater. At noon we stopped to stretch our legs and eat a quick sandwich then took off again. Late afternoon, when we reached the last branch of the Lauca River, the water was low enough for Barbie to stay on the motorcycle while Ron walked it across with the motor running. As usual, I waded across. After ten and a half hours of riding, we were glad to reach Chipaya. It was a great trip although the next day we all had bright red noses and my back was stiff for a few days.

Herman's Idol

As soon as we reached Chipaya, Herman asked, "Where's the idol I gave you when I entered God's Way? While you were away, my brother Paulino's baby died and my other brother was very sick. They said the idol was causing their sickness, so they stole some of my sheep for sacrifices and took me to court."

Paulino's wife also came, drunk and crying, accusing Ron of her baby's death. Fortunately, we hadn't destroyed the idol, so Ron found it and returned it to them.

Herman and his wife, Manuela, had entered God's Way, but when the going got rough they had gone back to the old ways, and Herman was accused of robbery. Now they were both very sick and were having all kinds of problems. When Herman consulted the shamans, they said, "God is punishing you for not continuing to follow him." This was an easy diagnosis because that's how their spirit gods worked. Herman had wanted to repent and return to the Lord, but Manuela said, "No," so they hadn't. A few days later, she died.

Albino and his family slept in our house that night because they were afraid Manuela's spirit would return to haunt them.

The Witness of a New Life

While we were in Chipaya, the Catholic Bishop came from Oruro to officially confirm Santiago as a Catholic leader. When Ron joined the community gathered in front of the Catholic church, Padre Amado said, "Come and sit with us," motioning to one of the chairs on the improvised platform.

First Santiago led the Chipayas in singing their favorite hymns and choruses in Spanish and Chipaya. After Santiago spoke, Feliciano told how his family had turned away from their idols to worship God. After the service Ron gave copies of the Chipaya Gospel of Mark and Bible stories to the Bishop, who seemed very pleased with them. Padre Amado already had copies.

Back to Civilization

Ron told the believers he was sorry the translation would be delayed again.

After a short stay in Chipaya, our motorcycle trip back to Oruro was easier as we plowed through the sand before the Yamaha motor got so hot. We made good time until a sandstorm caught us in the late afternoon. Barbie and I shut our eyes, but Ron had to squint enough to keep driving till we reached the Drain River where we ducked into the custom official's office. For an hour we watched thick clouds of sand and dust blow by, but finally we were able to cross the river on the raft and drive into Oruro. The next day we took the train to Cochabamba then Barbie and I flew back to Tumi while Ron took care of other group business in the city. It had been a great adventure!

Amy Ruth Joins our Family
One More Passenger for the Motorcycle

At Christmas we told the girls, "We're going to get you a talking, walking, eating, grow-hair doll in May!" Debbie, with a knowing smile, said, "I thought so!" Carla was incredulous: "You mean *us*?" and Barbie declared, "It's about time!" Most of her friends already had a baby sister or brother.

In April our family moved to Cochabamba. While waiting for Amy to arrive, and for a few weeks after, I filled in as hostess for our mission house.

Besides translating and helping other translators, Ron was asked to be city Coordinator, finding housing and Spanish tutors for new members, coordinating jobs for national employees and meetings for members, and being a general trouble-shooter. On the side, he gave lectures at the Center for Philosophic Studies on Chipaya culture and language. So for now, the Chipaya New Testament was on the back burner.

Amy Ruth arrived on May 16. We were all delighted with our new doll!

We'd been in Bolivia five years since our medical furlough, but decided to wait until Amy was a year old before spending a year in the States.

In July, when Amy was seven weeks old, a missionary pilot stationed in Cochabamba flew all six of us to Chipaya for a couple weeks. It took an hour and a half instead of a day by train and one or two days by truck. We all said, "Hurray!" In Chipaya, one of the girls' wicker doll baskets served as Amy's infant seat.

We were thankful the tide of persecution had turned, although the believers still faced challenges and some opposition.

Grandpa Sunday

Domingo was a ragged old grandpa who lived on the other side of town...

Domingo woke up stiff and cold from sleeping on the dirt floor of his little round hut. The wind blew in around his cactus-wood door. His homespun clothes were too ragged to keep him warm. He was hungry, too, but had nothing to eat. He stepped out over his high doorstep into the bright sunshine and sat down on the sand.

As he warmed up he thought, "I'm so hungry! I'm too old to work. Even my son has abandoned me. I'm so hungry..."

Then he remembered the outsiders who had come to live in his village and thought, "No one really knows why they've come. People say all kinds of things about them. But maybe they would give me some food." Hunger pulled him slowly to his feet and prodded him on his way to the missionaries' house across town.

Ron and I, the outsiders, gave him food that day. As he hungrily drank his soup from a tin cup, our three little girls watched him intently. Even in Chipaya they had never seen such rags, and such a wrinkled old face. They named him Grandpa Sunday since Domingo means Sunday.

Following that first visit a few years ago, old Grandpa came many times with dirty little bags for flour, corn meal, and sugar. We tried to talk to him about God, and play the Gospel records, but he was interested only in his flour and sugar.

Every time we left Chipaya we wondered if we would see him again.

Then our girls started praying for him every night: "Help Grandpa Sunday learn to love you before he dies." We said, "He's very old and we don't know how long he'll live, because no one gives him food when we're not there." So they prayed, "Help someone give him food. And help him learn to love you." We said, "The Chipayas don't usually talk to others about God, because to them it's like meddling in someone else's business." So then they prayed, "Help someone give him food and tell him about Jesus, so he can learn to love you before he dies."

The next time we went to Chipaya, crowds gathered at our house to see what medicines and new books we had brought. Suddenly the girls spotted Grandpa Sunday crossing the plaza, led by a little girl. Elated, they exclaimed, "He's still alive!" and as soon as he reached our house, they begged Ron, "Ask him! Ask him if he loves Jesus!" Ron said, "I can't do it when others are around. I'll have to wait till we're alone," so the girls went out to play in the sand.

One by one people left, as their curiosity was satisfied. Finally when they were alone, Ron asked him, "Grandpa, when are you going to enter God's Way?" A smile spread across his wrinkled face as he exclaimed, "God's way I have entered!" He added, "The Christian brothers brought me food, and they told me about God and asked if I wanted to enter God's Way. They told me what to say."

The words were a thrill and a rebuke to Ron and me, but pure delight to our girls.

It was still cold in his little hut. His clothes were more ragged than ever, although now he had a pair of long thermal underwear to wear underneath. Now when someone led him to our house, he was glad to fill his heart with hymns and Scripture, as well as his little sacks with food before Barbie led him home again.

The last time we saw Grandpa Sunday he begged us, "Please pray for my son Justino to enter God's Way."

Grandpa Sunday died four months later.

Reading or Communicating?

Ron wondered how we could best reach Chipaya with the Good News since it wasn't a reading culture. Older folks would never learn to read and many others lacked motivation, ability or practice.

Could the Porta-Teach tape players be the answer? They would at least be played till the batteries died. Gospel Recording records were good but they wore out too fast because the Chipayas used the same needles till they damaged the records. What about messages on tape? Young people would probably prefer a simplified Spanish Bible. Ron finally decided, "Instead of emphasizing reading, maybe we should focus on communicating."

With this in mind he spent many hours with Ceferino and Maximo, taping the Gospel of Mark, 1 John, and all the Bible stories, interspersed with hymns. Then we left tapes and two players so the believers could listen and lend them to others.

With Grandpa Sunday in mind, Ron wrote:

The Cassette

Oh, I want to hear God's voice in my ear
    speaking His message to me.
But all I see are black marks on a page
    that say nothing at all to me.

I could make those marks talk, if I only knew how.
They could tell me of God and of life.
They could free me from fear and from death.

But my head is so hard, it can't seem to learn
    or make sense of those marks in the book.
I look and I look but my eyes can't sort out
    the heads and the tails, and what they're about.

I struggle and try, I fail and I cry,
    "It's too hard for someone like me!"

But I still long to hear God's voice in my ear
    speaking His message to me.
Wait! Listen! I hear the Voice of The Book,
    God speaking the words of my tongue!

I've waited so long this message to hear,
    let me listen again and again.
It makes sense of my life and the world 'round about.
    Deep inside I know it's all true.

Now I don't need to puzzle the marks in a book.
I don't need to struggle and try.
My ears are just shaped for the words that I hear,
the words that I've used all my life.

My eyes are no good, but my ears – they know,
They remember each word, each phrase I hear.

Oh! How good to hear God's voice in my ear
speaking His message to me!
That's the way it will be in heaven, I'm sure.
I'll understand every word then,

But I can't wait 'til that day.
I need His Word *now*,
To save and to keep, to comfort and teach,
while walking the road here below.

Oh! How good to hear God's voice in my ear
speaking His message to me!

Approaching our Second Furlough

At the end of January Ron turned over his group responsibilities to another translator, hoping that when we returned in a year he would be free to focus on the Chipaya translation.

In February our travels took us from La Paz to Cochabamba in a commercial DC3 during a bad storm. The sky was dark and the wind tossed the plane around as we flew over the rugged mountains. The flight attendants buckled themselves into empty seats and grimly crossed themselves. As Ron and I prayed together, we wished we had made arrangements for our girls in case of such an emergency.

The minutes felt like hours.

It was getting dark when we finally bumped onto the unlighted runway in Cochabamba. We whispered, "Thank you, Lord! And please protect us till the Chipaya New Testament is finished."

Later, Ron, Amy and I flew to Chipaya for one more visit before furlough. One morning Ron discovered a man measuring the land our house was on. When West-Side had built the house and said we could live in it as long as we wanted, they never expected us to stay so long. We offered to pay for the house but they didn't want outsiders to own property in Chipaya. In the end, Maximo and his uncle bought it (with our help), agreeing to let us rent it back as long as we needed it till we finished translating the New Testament.

We knew that living in Chipaya would always be a challenge for the believers, but as we left them we were thankful the tide of persecution had turned. We encouraged them to listen often to the hymns, Scripture and Bible stories on the cassettes and share God's message of love and power with their families and friends.

As soon as our girls finished school, we flew to the U.S. During our furlough year we all had medical check-ups and Ron helped teach linguistic courses at SIL. He also summarized commentary information on Hebrews 11-13 while I finished a writing course. Our girls, meanwhile, were introduced to garage sales and public schools and we all enjoyed seeing family. As we shared the "Chipaya Challenge" we asked friends to pray for the believers and for us.

Back Home in Bolivia

By the next fall, 1972, we were back in Bolivia, determined to finish the New Testament in five years, but first Ron flew to Tumi for our annual conference where he was voted on to the Executive Committee again. We hoped administrative duties wouldn't take too much of his time.

While we were in the U.S., our mission had bought a Cessna 206 which was supercharged to fly in the altitude. Now Chipaya was eighty minutes away instead of three days.

At the same time, our mission said we needed to find other housing in Cochabamba because they needed the mission house for temporary guests. It had been so convenient to live there! I dreaded the thought of being blocks away from all our colleagues. We prayed for housing close by and Ron searched the newspapers for ads. What a happy surprise when we found an available house right across the street! The girls were near their friends and we could still eat our noon meal in the dining room, use the washing machines and work in the print shop! We planned to live and work mostly in Cochabamba so our girls could live at home, and only stay in the mission boarding school when Ron and I traveled to Chipaya.

After celebrating Carla and Barbie's birthdays, Ron headed for the *altiplano* where the Chipayas welcomed him – in happy contrast to a few years earlier. After eleven years, however, our straw roof was leaking badly. While the straw and the roof poles were off, Ron raised the back wall about three feet to give us a lot more useable space upstairs. This time we added aluminum roofing over the rafters and straw.

The three churches in Chipaya and two sister churches in Ayparavi served a total of fifty-two adult believers and sixty children including Aurelio, the boy featured in "Chipaya Christmas."

Zenobio's church was most active, and their teaching was based more on the Bible now. Ceferino had built a chapel but spent most of his time on town affairs. The Catholic group was growing. The believers had quit fighting each other and besides meeting for worship, they were seeking new ways to serve the community and to socialize. They were singing nineteen hymns and ten choruses now which we quickly printed in a new songbook. As the number of believers grew and others were openly interested in the Gospel, the line between believers and unbelievers was less clear.

During our absence, a Baha'i team had talked at length to all the Christian leaders, but without much success. They asked Maximo, "Why are you following the *gringo*?" He said, "I'm not following the *gringo*. I'm following God and His Word and I'll continue that way."

Two men had spent three or four weeks in Chipaya, studying the old customs. When they saw a Spanish New Testament in Feliciano's house they asked, "Did Señor Olson give you that?" He said, "No, I bought it in Oruro." They said, "It's not good. It's just man's ideas. You should go back to your ancestors' beautiful, good ways. That's what is best for you Chipayas." Feliciano said, "They aren't beautiful, good ways! They're bad ways with all the drinking and fighting! They lead us on a bad road to destruction!" The men finally left him alone, but made a point to visit all the believers.

Before leaving town they said, "We'll return next July or August to be in charge of a fiesta for one of your gods. We'll pay 1000 pesos to cover all the expenses." One of the believers said, "They'll probably just get everybody drunk then take a lot of pictures of them."

Ron told the Chipayas, "These people are interested in your customs so they can write about them, and be paid for it. They don't care if you're cold or sick or don't have electricity – but they wouldn't live this way themselves."

The Chipayas said that whenever visitors showed up they said, "We're friends of Señor Olson."

I Love You, But...

Once when I was by myself I started talking to Martina in English. I said...

I love you, Martina. I'm so glad you've entered God's Way. That's why Ron and I came to your village. There are a lot of believers now, and I don't even know them all. We've been gone for a long time, but now we're back after visiting our friends in the States and we're going to spend more time with you.

Ten years ago the first believers had a hard time. The whole community – including you – tried to run them out of town for leaving the old ways. Remember how angry you were when your nephew Maximo entered God's Way? They say you ranted and raved till you were out of your head. You had helped raise Maximo and couldn't stand it when he turned his back on everything you had taught him about worshipping and making sacrifices to the spirits.

But that was a long time ago. Now you, too, know that Jesus' sacrifice is the only one that counts. You've come a long way, Martina, and I'm so glad you're my sister now.

I love you, Martina...

But why don't you wait for me in the front room like everybody else does, instead of barging into the kitchen like you owned the place? Well, in a way I guess you do own it, since you bugged Maximo into selling you half of our house. But we're to live in it for five more years. You do know that, don't you?

I wish you wouldn't eye everything so enviously. I know my house is bigger and nicer than your little round hut, but it's really nothing compared to what we could have somewhere else. It's warmer, too. With our kerosene heater it's comfortable day and night, while water freezes in your house on winter nights. I guess we take for granted a lot of comforts you've never enjoyed. But as soon as we finish the New Testament we'll probably be gone and then the house will be all yours. So please be patient, okay?

And couldn't you have asked, at least, before laying your baby in Amy's bed? Did you see the wet spot she left? And there could have been fleas or lice in your blankets.

Your baby is awfully small and weak for a one-year-old. She whimpers and wants to nurse most of the time she's awake. They say quinoa isn't too good for a tiny baby, and there's not much else around here to eat, but couldn't you try to do something? It almost seems like you don't care.

And aren't you just a little bit selfish? Whenever I give other parents a piece of homemade bread they share it with their toddlers, but you eat all of yours and tell me to get some more for your kids. Wouldn't it be nicer to share?

I'm glad you like to sing hymns, and I'll try to help you learn them by heart since you can't read. But I'm all sung out right now. I feel like a record that can't go around another time. And besides, it's supper time, so why don't you go home? We served you (and your six kids) dinner, but that was because you carried pails of mud to help your husband mud our walls. And you just finished the last piece of our bread – didn't you hear Amy asking for some just after I gave it all to you?

I love you, Martina, but it's time for you to go home now...

* * * * *

That evening I prayed,

"And bless Martina, Father. You know I love her, but... What did you say? 'Love each other. Just as I have loved you...'? (John 13:34)

But how can I? She bugs me no end!

You say I'm not so perfect, either? Well, yes, I'm afraid you're right.

And you love me anyway? I'm sure glad you do.

But it's not going to be easy, Father.

You say I just need to be willing to love her, and you'll do the rest? Okay, I'm willing to try. But first let me start this little prayer all over again:

"And bless Martina, Father. You know I really *don't* love her, but I do want to. Please forgive me, and fill my heart with your love. Show me what I can do to express my love to her. And thank you for loving me, just like I am. Amen."

Warm Socks for Flory

Flory kept complaining, "My feet and legs ache from the cold." Mine would, too, if I went barefoot in freezing weather, so I said, "I'll teach you to knit so you can knit yourself some long wool socks." So she brought her yarn and I got her started. We were each knitting one sock. It was going so well that I had visions of starting a Ladies' Knitting Circle for Chipaya mothers to make warm socks for themselves and their children. But before I showed her how to knit the heel, her husband finished the sock she had been working on, then he showed me a pair he had made for himself previously. It aggravated me that he could knit for himself but wasn't willing to knit for her!

Ron reminded me that "Knitting is men's work. It's the men who knit all the caps for boys and men and baby girls."

So that ended my dream of a Ladies' Knitting Circle, but at least I knew that *one* lady in town had warm socks!

Grandpa Monday

Believe it or not, we now had a "Grandpa Monday!" since his first name, Lunalla, meant Little Moon. He was Amy's special friend. He was almost deaf from ear infections and he didn't seem interested in the Gospel, but we prayed that somehow the message of God's love would reach his heart, as it had reached Grandpa Sunday.

Family Time in Chipaya

During Christmas vacation our whole family flew to Chipaya for three weeks, and Elaine, the daughter of a missionary pilot, spent a week with us. We showed Bible filmstrips with a pack of twenty-seven batteries. It was a new experience for Chipaya viewers and they loved to watch them. To accompany the songs, Barbie played a harmonica, Carla and Debbie played recorders, and Elaine played her flute. They got a lot of practice when the Chipayas sang all the stanzas in Chipaya, Spanish and Aymara!

When we went to the river for a picnic, Ron took all five girls – A (Amy), B, C, D and E – on the motorcycle at once! F (yours truly) walked part way till Ron came back for me!

As soon as school let out in May, we all spent a month in Chipaya. Debbie helped twenty-eight children sew rag dolls, Barbie learned to spin, and all three girls learned to weave, Chipaya style. Since it was winter, they also enjoyed sliding on the river ice.

Speeding up Translation

To speed up all the translation programs in Bolivia, Ron led a workshop in Tumi in the book of James. All the translators and language helpers studied a chapter or section together in the morning, then each language group translated it into their language in the afternoon. At the end of the workshop, the book of James was in first draft in nine languages.

In Chipaya, Feliciano was busy searching the Scriptures for his answers. Many evenings he came asking Ron, "What does the Bible teach about praying? Divinations? Dreams? Tithing? Drinking? How to live the Christian life?" He had made a profession some years earlier, but drinking had pulled him back to the old ways for a while. Now he wanted to learn more about God and the Bible.

Zenobio's group was building a larger church, about twelve by forty-five feet, with an aluminum roof, and doors and windows from Oruro. They assessed themselves from 100 to 1000 pesos. The one owing 1000 had already paid 900.

The believers wanted the New Testament right away. We said, "We'll finish as soon as possible, maybe even next year, but we'll need your help." When they found errors in the hymnbook, Ron said, "It's too bad you didn't catch those errors before it was printed. You'll really have to check the Scriptures carefully so that doesn't happen in the New Testament." After thinking about it for a while, they agreed. Ron tried to check Acts with Florencio while we were in Chipaya but as usual there were so many interruptions, they finally gave up.

Florencio in Cochabamba

We were delighted when Florencio, a sharp young Christian, came to work with Ron in Cochabamba for two months. They worked from morning till evening. The first day they translated seventy verses in eight hours!

It was fig season, and Florencio couldn't stop eating them. He said, "These are really sweet! I never tasted them before." Ron said, "Help yourself – the tree is loaded!" The next day Florencio had to excuse himself every little while to run to the men's room, but he still kept enjoying the figs, as we all did.

Whenever Florencio was tired of sitting or felt drowsy, he'd stand up and walk slowly around the table while they kept translating. In ten weeks they did the first draft of Luke, Acts, Thessalonians through Philemon, and 1 Corinthians! Now we had half the New Testament in first draft! They worked full days for six weeks, and then half days for the last month when Florencio was feeling tired. Ron dreamed of finishing the New Testament the next year, 1974.

Ron still needed to check the translation carefully against the Greek New Testament for correctness, but we were well on the way and it was going great!

Now that we had more books translated, we printed a pocket-sized booklet of selected verses.

When Guzman, another young believer, came to Cochabamba, he and I translated stories about Abraham, Isaac, Jacob and Joseph. My head was swimming after only two weeks. I didn't know how Ron could concentrate for so long.

Florencio said he would spend January and February, the summer vacation months, translating with Ron in the city again. He also said, "I want to be a substitute teacher next year. Would that be good?" Ron said, "It might or it might not. If it means you'd have less time for the church and getting the Scriptures in Chipaya, it might not be good."

The next Christmas Ron's brother, Dennis, and his family came from Peru for a couple weeks. The cousins had a great time together. When we came home from taking them to the airport, we found Ceferino knocking at our gate, ready to start translating. What timing! It had taken him five days to travel from Chipaya because of heavy rains in the *altiplano*.

The Gospel Spreads

When we first arrived in the Chipaya area thirteen years earlier, there were very few Evangelical churches anywhere on the *altiplano*, but now the Gospel was spreading like wildfire among the Aymaras. When a soccer team came from Huachacalla to play against Chipaya, five players were Baptists and one was a Pentecostal. One of the players was Ismael, the Aymara neighbor boy who used to play with our girls. He bought two Bibles and New Testaments and one of the school teachers also bought a New Testament.

Ceferino learned four new Aymara hymns at a Christian conference during Carnival and when he and Maximo spent a night at our house, they helped Ron translate one of them into Chipaya. Staying overnight gave Ceferino and Maximo a good chance to talk late into the night and again early in the morning. On Sunday morning Ceferino, Maximo and Ron recorded fifteen hymns and two choruses on thirty-minute cassettes. Later Ron made seventeen copies of the cassette tapes to distribute to the believers.

Ron used the Christmas story for the believers to practice reading.

It was exciting to see new believers among the Aymaras and also among the Chipayas, now that God was speaking to them in their own language.

* * * * *
Now God Speaks Chipaya

The Reverend Ronald D. Olson and his wife, Frances, spent their three-month honeymoon in the Mexican jungles, training for pioneer living. After further work in linguistics and a course in Spanish the Olsons went to live among the Chipaya Indians on the high barren plateau which lies between ranges of the Andes. Mrs. Olson's parents retired this year after forty-two years of service with the Central American Mission.

* * * * *

"The spirits told me, 'We will punish Chipaya this year unless everyone joins in the Carnival procession and rituals!'" boldly announced the head shaman. There was stunned silence in the town meeting of the highland village in Bolivia, South America. Then someone echoed, "That's right. *Everyone* has to take part – even the evangelicals." Everyone seemed to agree, till slowly and deliberately another Chipaya man spoke up. "Listen, brothers," he said thoughtfully, "if the spirits punish Chipaya, they'll punish *you*. God will take care of *us*. We can't take part in the procession and rituals because we aren't the demons' people anymore."

The town hall buzzed with consternation, but the believers stood firm. Exasperated but helpless, the community finally resolved that every man must defend himself against the spirits as best he could. God's people would have to pray to Him for protection and the others would have to try to appease the demons with extra animal sacrifices.

As the Indians finally scattered in the wee hours of the morning, they pulled their homespun cloaks tightly around them. The night was beautiful, but bitterly cold. Shivering, Florencio recalled the old days when he had been a slave to the evil spirits, groaning under the burden of blood sacrifices and rituals, helpless before the capricious demons. Not many years ago, as leader of the Lauca fiesta, he had slaughtered sheep, pigs and llamas to appease the blood-thirsty god of the Lauca River which watered their arid farmlands. In deference to the evil gods he had drunk and danced till existence was a blur. Then, with muddled mind he had beaten his faithful wife and collapsed beside her in a stupor.

Their two little children, frightened, hungry and cold, had huddled together in their dark mud hut and cried themselves to sleep.

But things were different now. Florencio was free from the old gnawing fear of the vengeful spirits, free to serve a loving God and live a good life. A sense of deep peace overwhelmed him, but even in his *smooth heart* there was a tinge of sadness. Oh that all his Chipaya brothers would enter God's Way! If only they could understand His ways and recognize His power! Now that a third of the villagers were believers, even the *kaka* didn't come around very often. This mysterious red glow had often wandered around the grave houses and other holy ground, and occasionally visited someone's home.

Then even the strong-hearted spent sleepless nights in terror, waiting for calamity to strike. "Why don't we see the *kaka* like we used to?" the unbelievers wondered. Florencio knew. His God was ruler of heaven and earth – even the powers of evil fled before Him.

Walking home, Florencio scanned the sky, spangled with stars from horizon to horizon. His God had put them there! He smiled as the words of a Chipaya hymn rose in his heart: "In the above-God's hand are we. God the Father is right beside me." He loved to sing. All Chipayas do. He wondered why their fiesta tunes didn't have words. He had never sung till he sang God's songs. Even the unbelievers liked the Gospel songs, especially those with original highland tunes. The songs were good; so was God's Word. God's Word – how he wished he had it in his language. "We need it; that's real food," he said to himself.

When he got home he pushed open his cactus-wood door. Without even changing his clothes, he curled up on the sheepskins, pulling a heavy woolen blanket over himself. When he woke, his wife Emiliana was already starting a fire in the mud stove.

"Before the town meeting last night I was talking to Pajk Jila," said Florencio. (That's what they call the linguist-translator, meaning "big brother.") "He asked if I'd go with him to Cochabamba to help translate the New Testament. It's impossible to get it done here with so many interruptions. I'd be gone for two or three months at a time." He looked inquiringly at Emiliana, but her tiny braids curved down and hid her face as she leaned over to blow the fire.

"Two or three months," she thought, "to tend the sheep and keep track of the llamas all by myself; two or three months to collect llama dung for fuel, and walk out to check the quinoa fields, leaving the little boys alone for several hours…but then – God could speak to us in our own language!"

She looked up and answered, "Yes. Go. I'll get along. We need God's Word in our language." Then she bent over the fire again.

And so it was that Florencio came to Cochabamba last year. In an hour and fifteen minutes he flew high over the barren plateau, over the Andes Mountains and into the world of streets and stores. After a few weeks of concentrated translation work he said, "My back and my legs have often been tired, but never my head. Why does it feel so heavy and tired?" He was finding out that translating is hard work, struggling to understand what the Scriptures really mean and then straining to express them clearly and accurately in Chipaya. But putting his weary head to work again, Florencio asserted, "I want God to speak *good* Chipaya!"

This year he came back again "to help God speak Chipaya" – what an awesome task! This time the rains had begun and it took him five difficult days to travel to Cochabamba. But God had lit a fire in his heart and he came. Again he worked till his weary head ached, but never once said, "It's too much. I want to go home."

He knows there is still a lot of checking and revising to do before the New Testament can be printed and distributed, but he is living for the day when he can say, "Now God speaks Chipaya!"⁴

Just Another Mary?

On my way to visit Martina, my sick friend, I saw Maria…

I first saw her crouched outside her little round hut. She was on her knees and elbows on the hard, dry ground, trying to absorb the last warm rays of the afternoon sun. All I could see was her ragged homespun dress, tiny tousled braids, bare feet and wrinkled hands.

I said, "Hello, Grandma. I've come to visit you." Slowly she sat up and turned toward me but her sunken eyes couldn't see who had spoken. Her dark brown face was a mass of wrinkles. I repeated my greeting and sat down beside her, taking her thin, shriveled hand in mine.

"Do you have a husband?" I asked gently.

"He died long ago."

"Children?"

"One of them lives out in the country. One usually lives in town."

"Who cooks your food?"

"My son, but he's away. Do you have food? I'm hungry."

I said I'd bring some, then added, "Grandma, I want to tell you about Jesus. He loves you. He wants to give you new life so you can live with God in heaven."

"Are you Jesus?" she asked.

"No. Jesus is God's Son. There's one true God and Jesus is His Son." Then I read John 3:16 from our little memory verse booklet, repeating the phrases over and over. She echoed them slowly, in a low, wondering voice. Then I sang the chorus of "Jesus Loves Me" till her weak quavering voice joined mine.

Every day for a week, I visited her, taking a piece of bread or a bit of meat. I said, "Grandma, Jesus loves you and He died to take the punishment for your sins. But you have to believe what He says and enter God's Way so you can live with Him in heaven after you die."

"I want to die. I'm tired of living," she said wearily.

"But Grandma, unless you enter God's Way you can't live with God. You will have to be punished for your sin. Forever. Don't you want to enter God's Way?"

But it was all so new and strange. She spoke slowly as though groping in the darkness. "I'm so old. I just can't understand."

Then the week was gone. "Grandma, tomorrow I have to go to Cochabamba."

"I'll never see you again" she said sadly.

"If you enter God's Way, you'll go to heaven and we *will* see each other again."

"But I'm so old. I just can't understand," she repeated wearily.

So I finally had to say goodbye, but promised to have the Chipaya believers visit her and explain it all so she could understand...

Then I went on to visit Martina once more. Tomas, Maxine and a few other believers were in her little round house. At the open doorway I said, "I've come to visit." They said, "Come in. Sit down." I stepped over the high threshold and sat down on the sheep skins beside them. They asked, "What news do you have?"

I said, "I've been visiting Grandma Maria, and taking her some food, and telling her about Jesus. I told her, 'You should enter God's Way;' but she says, 'I'm too old. I don't understand.'"

They sort of smiled and said, "Yes, she's very old and will probably die soon."

I said, "You need to tell her how to enter God's Way."

They said, "But she hasn't been interested, and she's so old!"

I said, "That's exactly *why* you need to visit her. She's going to die soon, and then it will be too late."

When they saw me crying they whispered to each other, "She really feels for her, doesn't she?"

I said, "Jesus really feels for her, too. He loves her and wants her to be in heaven with Him. Please visit her and tell her how to enter God's Way, before she dies. And please take her some food."

Caring about old people was new for the Chipayas, but they knew I was serious and they promised to visit her. The next day we flew back to Cochabamba where we asked our Wycliffe family to pray that the believers would reach out to her.

Returning from a quick trip to Chipaya a couple months later, Ron said, "After we left Chipaya, the believers met in Grandma Mary's little round hut. They sang and prayed far into the night, and each one told how they had entered God's Way. Finally she said, 'Now I understand,' and she prayed to enter God's Way. Three days later she was welcomed into God's Town."

Solving Medical Mysteries?

When school was out, our mission doctor and his daughter, Pam, flew to Chipaya with Ron and Debbie. The girls were the designated cooks for the week. Pam's other job was to clean the area when folks needed a shot. Her dad said, "I didn't realize what a big job I gave her. It took a lot of cotton and alcohol!" The doctor hoped to solve some of our medical mysteries, but unfortunately, it was hard to diagnose the cause of their aches and pains. He was very surprised to find few parasites other than pork tape worms (for which there was no treatment available). He said, "Apparently it is just so barren that not even the bugs grow there!" He gave the Mantoux test for tuberculosis to one hundred twelve people, including sixty-five school children, but much to our surprise very few tested positive. It was a good visit in spite of not solving many mysteries.

Concerning the believers, the doctor commented, "You get in an area like that where it is a very tightly structured community, plus this very active idol worship which obviously has to do with Satan worship… To see that there are actually believers in Chipaya is really something – very encouraging against overwhelming odds. It is really tremendous."

Padre Amado's Conference

We were thrilled to see how Florencio remembered passages he had helped translate, and was applying them to life. When Padre Amado gave a message to the Chipaya community, Florencio translated for him. The priest's message was very short whereas Florencio's version was much longer. Later, Padre Amado asked Ron, "What was he saying? His message was a lot longer than mine." Ron said, "He was explaining what you said with examples from Scripture." Padre Amado was satisfied.

Padre Amado told the Chipayas, "Make a list of questions you'd like answered, then send delegates to a conference where we'll answer them." The believers made a list of questions, but said, "We need these answered tomorrow, right here so everybody can hear." So discussions started the next day. The first question, "How should a Christian live?" was thrown back to the Chipayas. It ended up with believers telling how God had changed their lives. The next question was, "Can we drink or not?" They listed the bad consequences of drinking, but no one mentioned anything from the Bible.

When the topic of baptism came up, Padre Amado said, "We baptized over one hundred babies a month ago, but where are they now?" The believers said, "You should suspend all baptisms for three years while you preach the Bible, and then those who really believe and show it by their lives can be baptized."

The next day Maximo and Feliciano asked Ron what the Bible said about those topics, and about taking part in the fiestas. They read passages from 1 Corinthians 6 and 10 where it says "You cannot drink from the cup of the Lord and from the cup of demons, too" (1 Cor. 10:21). Drinking at the fiestas was in honor of whatever spirit god they were worshipping. Ron said, "Unless you get your answers from the Bible, it's just your word against someone else's."

"Could Lightning Make Her Sick?"

Albino and Sabina's two-month-old baby girl was very sick. Sabina came to visit, and sat on the floor, as Chipaya women preferred to do. After a while she asked, "Could lightning make Rebeca sick?" I asked "Is that what the Chipayas say?" She said "Lightning was flashing around our country home a few days ago. The people say that's a bad omen. Then Rebeca got sick." I said, "A lot of people are sick, and the sickness goes from sick people to well people, then they get sick, too." Looking sadly at her baby,

Sabina said, "They say lightning can enter your body and make you sick. All my baby girls have died – all five of them – but my boys haven't died." I said, "Let's ask God to protect her and heal her. Amy is sick, too, and my husband is giving her shots. He has medicine that would probably help Rebeca get well." After a long pause she repeated, "All my baby girls have died. There was a lot of lightning." I asked, "Would you like some medicine?" She didn't answer. She seemed far away. Maybe my broken Chipaya phrases weren't very convincing. Pretty soon she stood up and said, "I'm going now," as she pulled her cape over her head and shoulders, to protect little Rebeca on her back. I said, "You may go," and opened the door. She stepped out into the cold wind and was gone. My heart ached for her. She never came for medicine. Maybe after losing so many baby girls she lost hope. But in spite of not giving her any medicine, little Rebeca survived and recovered.

Four years later there was a siege of flu with terrible headaches and weakness. When almost all the medicines were gone, and we were preparing to leave the village, Albino came saying, "Rebeca is dying. She has stopped breathing and there's no pulse." Ron gave her the last dose of antibiotics and prayed with them for her healing.

We were so thankful to see her alive and well when we returned a couple months later.

Paper Bells

On another visit there was little medical work, except for treating four-year-old Julia who caught her heel in her dad's bicycle spokes. Her dad, Eduardo, said, "She kept crying and begging, 'Take me to Tall Brother! He will cure me!'" Julia was a brave little trooper as Ron cleaned and bandaged her heel and Amy, who was about her same age, was very impressed. While Ron treated her, Amy colored and cut out some paper bells. When she handed them to her new little friend, Julia responded with a big smile.

In the past, Julia's dad had been a very filthy-mouthed, ornery, and unpleasant character to have around. He would sit in our house criticizing us and everything he saw, speaking just low enough so we couldn't hear everything he said. He was very different now, interested in what the Bible said, and very loving and gentle with his little daughter.

Visiting Ayparavi

On our third Sunday in Chipaya, Ron, Amy and I rode the motorcycle to worship with the believers in Ayparavi. We heard that most Chipayas in Ayparavi were believers and the Gospel was spreading from their church to surrounding Aymara villages. All the authorities were believers, as well as next year's appointees.

Zenobio had started the church in Ayparavi using the Chipaya songbook and Spanish Bible. The schools now boasted six grades so children were reading more Spanish, and young men who worked on farms in Chile during the summer months also knew more Spanish. Most adults wore Spanish-style clothes instead of the typical homespun and acculturation was speeding up.

Houses were rectangular instead of round and the believers were building a church, paying for everything themselves, including the aluminum roof. We gave them money to help pay for windows and a door. Inside they had an adobe platform, a couple chairs, a small table with a blue plastic tablecloth and even a couple STP cans holding bright plastic flowers!

The women spread their large square capes on the dirt floor for sitting along the left wall while the men sat along the opposite wall on adobes or cactus-wood benches. As the honored guest, I was given sheepskins to sit on. Amy lay on one and played in the dirt during the three-hour meeting conducted in Chipaya, Spanish and Aymara. At the end of the service an Aymara family said they wanted to follow God. Aurelio's brother and mother said they were interested in God's Way, but not ready to make a commitment yet.

After the service, we hung a heavy, dark cloth over the doorway so Ron could show Bible filmstrips. They really enjoyed the stories. By three in the afternoon the quinoa dinner served by Francisco's family, our former neighbors, tasted very good. It was nice to visit with them now as believers and see that mischievous Mateo had grown up to be a nice young man.

* * * * *

While Ron and Florencio were translating in Cochabamba in February, 1974, a contest was going on in Chipaya...

Contest on Mount Carmel – The God Who Answers

Rain. Rain. Rain. As it fell, the rivers rose. The Chipayas watched in dismay, wondering how to save their crops. They diverted the main streams and sacrificed sheep to appease the angry spirits, but still the rain fell and the water, like a flood, approached from the north. In a couple weeks all their crops were washed away. Still the water rose, surrounding the town, converting the town square into a lake and the streets into rivers. Adobe houses, standing in water, began to collapse. About thirty town houses fell and many more of their country homes. Without food, the sheep, llamas and pigs were starving.

Frantically, the prophets of Baal prayed to their gods and sacrificed more animals to the idols, the ancestor spirits, and any other spirits they thought might be offended. The priests of Baal undressed the idols and set them on the wet ground so they would feel the cold and stop the rain. But there was no reply. No voice. No answer.

The rains continued and the water kept rising. For two weeks everything was under water. They feared for their lives. Finally, in desperation, the town officials and many others came to the believers, begging them to pray to God to see if he could stop the rain and save them from the flood. This was Sunday morning, February 17, 1974.

Lightning crackled in the dark sky and thunder rolled as the community waded through town to the big Catholic Church. They all crowded inside, cramming the largest meeting place in town. First the believers sang hymns then Elijah – I mean Maximo – urged the people to abandon their idols and turn to God, adding, "Don't be afraid because God is going to help us." Then they prayed, some in the big church and some in their own churches: "Father God, show your power by stopping the rain and saving us from this flood. Show the people that you hear us and you have power over everything."

In the early afternoon when they waded back to their soggy homes, the sky was still dark and the rain still falling. But slowly the rain stopped and before sundown the sky was clearing. That night the stars shone again for the first time in three weeks. Monday dawned clear and almost cloudless. The water began to recede.

In speechless wonder and relief the Chipayas watched as day after day the sun shone and the water went down. By the end of the week their town was dry! Those who had ridiculed or talked against the believers were silenced. "Surely they *are* in touch with God!" they admitted in amazement, and ten families in the main town of Chipaya turned from idols to serve the living God.

Then Maximo and other church leaders cycled fifteen miles to the Chipaya community of Ayparavi. On Saturday they announced,

"If any of you want to accept the Lord, discuss it with your family tonight. Tomorrow we'll visit you." So on Sunday, after singing and praying in the main church, they visited each home, explaining the way of salvation from God's Word. And the results? Seven families and some single men accepted the Lord, leaving only six families in Ayparavi to follow *Baal*.

And so the God of Elijah demonstrated His power again. The Chipayas have seen His power in stopping the rain and in saving them. Let's pray that they will also know His power in living a new life pleasing to Him.[5]

The rest of the story...

The believers had offered to be responsible for the quinoa fields that year, but the community said, "No!" In January, Sebastian, who was in charge of sacrificing to Lauca Mallcu, the river spirit, told the believers, "Each of you need to contribute a case of beer or soft drinks for the fiesta." They said, "No way." He retorted, "The Lauca spirit is very powerful. If you don't worship him, he will punish you. He's the one who brings water so we can exist."

When the rains persisted and the river was threatening the crops, the believers asked Sebastian, "Is the Lauca Mallcu helping you? Is he bringing enough rain?!"

As the water rose, Sebastian stopped talking against the believers. Since Vicente, the shaman mayor, was out of town, Sebastian was totally responsible for appeasing the spirits. Finally, in desperation, he and the community leaders begged the believers to pray to their God.

That was when the God of Elijah demonstrated his power! The Chipayas saw his power and even Tomas, the shaman, entered God's Way!

Since Chipaya families entered God's Way together, that meant that now his wife, Maxine, my special friend, was a believer, as well as Damiana, their teenage daughter! Now there was talk about "... when most Chipayas are believers..." and "...when the big church is cleaned out..." meaning no more images, blood sacrifices or other paraphernalia!

Of Death and Life

Toribia's mother, a very old lady, was very sick. She was one of those who entered God's Way after the flood. Her family said that just before she died she raised her arms saying, "Lord Jesus, take me, take me." Most of her family members were Christians but some weren't, so the funeral was a mixture of customs. First the believers sang almost all the Chipaya hymns as well as some in Spanish and Aymara, and read Scripture. At that time the cross was not a Christian symbol, so they made a wooden burial marker in the shape of a triangle representing the Trinity, inscribed with "Jesus said, I am the resurrection and the life" (John 11:25).

Then the unbelievers took over, placing the head of a sacrificed sheep near her head. They sprinkled her body with alcohol and coca leaves, praying to the spirits. Then they wrapped her body in a blanket and carried it with ropes. In the cemetery, the entire family built a small tomb around and over her body, as was the custom, but they didn't leave the usual hole for food and drink offerings to her spirit. The family served hard candies and soda pop to all those present, instead of the usual coca leaves and alcohol.

Walking back to town from the cemetery with Toribia, I tried to comfort her, reminding her that her Mom was now in heaven with Jesus – alive, happy and well.

* * * * *

One day when Tomas came by and asked, "Do you know me?" it brought back a flood of memories...

Tomas, You're a Miracle!

An ex-shaman confronted and changed by the power of God.

Tomas, brother, it's nice to see you again. You ask if we know you? What a question! We'd recognize you anywhere. Anytime. But it's a long time since you've come to visit. When we first came to your village fifteen years ago you visited us often.

You remind me of Zacchaeus. Short. Especially without the tall white felt hat that all the other Chipaya men wear. And even way back when we first came, you were a chief. Not a chief of tax collectors, but a chief of shamans. You've always admired power, haven't you? Power over people and situations; power over the evil spirits.

And you've always had to be different. Remember the first picture we took of your town band? The other men all wore their white hats and held a flute or a set of panpipes, and there you stood in the front row with your dirty blue baseball cap and *three* panpipes. Not one but three. That was you, Tomas, never content with normal trappings.

You were smart. We knew it from the beginning, but we still couldn't believe it when you picked up that booklet a few minutes ago and read the Christmas story straight through! No one else ever jumped from reading Spanish to reading Chipaya as easily as you. Yes, most of the letters are similar to Spanish but some combinations are very unusual. Yet you read it straight through and hardly hesitated.

Remember when your wife Maxima [Maxine] washed clothes for me that first year? You weren't happy about her coming, but she was unusually fearless, open and enjoyed visiting the foreigners, while most Chipaya women were afraid of us. And I enjoyed visiting your little round house, the only native house I entered for a long time. Every few days I used to crouch to step through your low doorway, sit on the dirt floor, then bluntly ask, "Maxima, do you want to wash clothes? Please come." One day you scolded me for being so blunt and dictated long sentences of polite ways to request help. Maybe we could have been better friends if I had made myself memorize them instead of feeling offended and defensive of my first Chipaya phrases.

And you really thought something must be wrong with me if I couldn't nurse my baby like every other mother did. Who ever heard of feeding a baby from a bottle?! Chipaya mothers had plenty of milk for their babies and even some to spare for the lambs whose mothers happened to die. Yes, we knew that. Maxima herself used to nurse her little girl *and* her lamb right in our house.

I'll never forget the day Maxima invited me for a food gift. She said to come to your house about sundown. It was Christmas time, but you didn't know about Christmas in those days. When I reached your house, Maxima was excitedly distributing things for the relatives to carry: quinoa soup in a square five-gallon can, fluffy steamed quinoa in a large cloth, a basket of clay bowls, a few withered flowers from the far-off hills. If I had realized what was ahead, I never would have gone. But I'm glad I didn't know. Your family, like all Chipaya families, was performing the fertility rites for the flocks. And Tomas, I watched in horror as you sacrificed two lambs that evening, and sprinkled the blood over the flocks. You also sprinkled blood on the ground in honor of the spirits and demons. When the lukewarm soup was finally served I couldn't eat it. I felt sick all over. That was fourteen Christmases ago. Now you finally know that Christmas really is God's own Son coming to be the Sacrifice to end all sacrifices.

The next year some of the townspeople left the old ways to enter God's way. The rest of you didn't like that and did everything in your power to make them recant or get out of town. Sort of like the early Christians, only they had nowhere to flee. But you couldn't make them turn back, could you? A new Power seemed to protect and sustain them. Then you wouldn't let Maxima wash clothes for me anymore, nor even come to visit. And you didn't want me in your house anymore. I was sorry. Not just because I missed Maxima's help (no one else ever took her place), but I missed her friendship. She was my first friend way back then, but you didn't trust her near us anymore.

On one occasion when we flew out of the village, we learned you had cursed our plane and arrogantly announced we would crash before ever reaching Cochabamba. What did you think when we returned a couple of months later? Did you feel cheated? Angry because your curses had been ineffective – because your power had failed?

Meanwhile the church was growing in spite of persecution, and you lost many of your followers. You must have been enraged as they escaped from under your power. Ten years slipped by. To us you symbolized the old ways: the bondage to the evil spirits and the hopelessness of the old life. Twice Maxima came secretly to our house at night for medicine when your little children were very ill – when the spirits refused to be appeased. Did you send her for help when your power couldn't heal them? Or did she come without your knowing? We were sorry when your little son died. Did his death undermine your trust in the spirits – your power with them?

Then came the flood. Crops were washed away. Water covered the pastures. Houses sagged and toppled. You shamans desperately sacrificed sheep, more sheep, llamas and pigs to the spirits of nature, to the saints, demons, ancestors, and all the spirits you ever heard of. Yet for three more weeks the water kept rising till you feared for your lives. Didn't your gods hear? Didn't they care? Where was their power?

Finally in desperation the community leaders begged the believers to pray to their God. It was like the contest on Mount Carmel between Elijah and the prophets of Baal. The believers prayed. The rain stopped. The stars appeared. Then the sun shone. In a week your town was dry. That was real power, wasn't it, Tomas? No one could deny it. And for the first time in history Chipaya believers took the initiative to approach their brothers and ask them if they didn't want to serve this true and powerful God.

You always worshipped power, and now you were confronted by a Power greater than all the evil spirits you had served so faithfully. Was that what finally made you switch allegiance? All the time you were seeking the Greatest Power and finally you were convinced? When your Christian brothers introduced you to him, you met him face to face and fell at his feet!

Now the miracle of the flood seems nothing compared to the miracle that has transformed your life. Your restless eyes used to flash with distrust and deceit. Now they are smiling with a new light. Your heart so choked by evil and hate has been set free to sing a new song and serve a loving God.

You ask if we recognize you. How could we help it? It's you – baseball cap and all – but not the same old you. Tomas, you're a miracle![6]

Chipaya Translation Speeds Up

After conference, Ron helped four translators write up grammar materials for their languages, and helped others with linguistic problems, translation questions, or in whatever way they needed.

Back in Cochabamba, my project was to tabulate all the theological terms and abstract nouns in the translated material and list the ways we had expressed them.

The next rainy season when Florencio came again to translate with Ron, we were praying they would both stay healthy and alert to finish Matthew and John by the end of February. What a joy when they translated Matthew, John *and* Romans!

In mid-May, 1974, with Florencio's eager help, the first draft of the Chipaya New Testament was finished! Florencio had also written seventeen new songs, and even typed them out before showing them to us.

"Correcting Florencio's Work"

As soon as we returned to Chipaya, Feliciano wanted to "correct Florencio's work." He tended to be literal, but was helpful. When visitors asked, "What are you doing?" He'd say, "I'm correcting Florencio's work." He told Ron, "I probably know Spanish better than anyone else in Chipaya." In spite of being a bit proud, Feliciano was a capable and determined worker. Ron admitted, "I guess we aren't perfect yet, either!" As Ron read the Chipaya translation, Feliciano followed along in the Spanish New Testament to check what had been done. He hadn't been a believer very long, but was already reading through the Spanish New Testament for the second time.

By the second week, Feliciano's head hurt, but he insisted on working full time. He might have been working for the pay, but he was also becoming familiar with God's Word in Chipaya. He was very out-going and we expected him to be a church leader some day. During the three weeks we were in Chipaya, he made some good suggestions as he and Ron read through Matthew, Luke, John and Acts. This was the first time Ron had ever had consistent translation help in the village and it was wonderful! Ron's biggest challenge was how to translate figures of speech and parables in Luke. Translation was hard work, striving to understand God's Word in the Greek language then express it naturally in Chipaya.

Approaching the Finish Line!

After a consultant checked our translation, we needed representatives from all three Chipaya churches to make sure it was clear and natural-sounding. Ron suggested that some leaders work full-time revising the New Testament instead of planting crops. We were thankful when Florencio chose to help translate instead of being a teacher's aide the following school year.

In the fall of 1974, Ron was on schedule to finish the New Testament, using the Greek New Testament to check his translation for accuracy.

I had finally finished my six-year project of adapting the David C. Cook illustrations, which gave us artwork for Bible stories from Genesis to Revelation. Now I was preparing a booklet about Jesus Christ's power over sickness, nature, sin, spirits, death, etc., based on the Gospel of Mark.

That fall we flew to Chipaya with a little booklet of selected verses and a new songbook of sixty Chipaya hymns, each with its Spanish or Aymara counterpart. The afternoon we arrived, we sold sixty hymnbooks and twenty Spanish New Testaments. Over the weekend the count climbed to one hundred ten hymnbooks, fifty-six New Testaments and four Bibles. I enjoyed singing with the ladies even if it meant singing till I was hoarse, because that is how they learned the songs when they couldn't read. We ordered a hundred more New Testaments with Psalms for Zenobio's group.

We printed verses on calendars and Christmas cards which everybody liked to hang in their houses. We also took booklets or leaflets in Spanish. The Chipayas especially liked the booklet about "The Heart of Man," which showed Jesus chasing wild animals, which represented evil traits, out of their hearts.

In December, Florencio and Maximo read through Luke, 1 Corinthians, and four short New Testament books with Ron. Then we used a hectograph to print the Christmas story on five pages of colored pictures. Back in Cochabamba, Ron had another translator check 1 Corinthians so we could print it right away, since the Chipaya believers faced many of the same problems as the believers in Corinth. Our main challenge now was how to translate *the kingdom of God, glory, believers*, and other key terms.

That year, when the Chipaya authorities asked for aid from government officials in Oruro, the Prefect said, "You're stupid to keep living out there! Every year you come looking for aid. You should move to the lowlands. I'll talk to the officials in La Paz about giving you a piece of land somewhere else." With the government talking about relocating the Chipayas, Ron said, "It's more urgent than ever to finish the New Testament quickly because if they move, they will need God's help to steady them in all their new adjustments."

A Chipaya School Teacher?

Chipaya was a *central* school now, boasting eight grades for the first time, and growing in numbers. We were glad to learn that one of the eight teachers was a Christian.

Ron told the director, "You should appoint a Chipaya man to help teach the first and second graders until they learn some Spanish." When the director agreed, Ron offered, "If you make an official request and get your supervisor in Oruro to approve it, SIL will help out in La Paz to make it happen." Florencio said, "They have already asked me to teach one religion lesson a week in each class, and I'm willing to teach this year, even without pay." Ron said, "Great! You could teach the Bible stories we've printed and maybe use the songbooks to teach Chipaya reading. You could sell songbooks to the students for one peso (about eight cents)." Before long Florencio was an official teacher.

When the teachers asked Ron to translate the national anthem, he translated the first verse and chorus. After checking it with the Chipaya authorities, everyone was pleased and the next year the second graders sang it in the closing program. Ron also gave magazines and another used typewriter to the school, and took pictures of students and teachers on "Children's Day."

New Horizons

One Sunday the Catholics celebrated a birthday. The birthday family prepared a meal for the whole group, and some folks even brought gifts of cheese, quinoa, etc. The idea probably came from Florencio who was with us in Cochabamba when we invited mission friends for cake and ice cream on Ron's birthday.

Another Sunday both sides of town had a long important meeting. The outcome was that they would no longer schedule town meetings or community work on Sunday because the unbelievers were tired of waiting for the believers to finish their meetings. From then on Sunday would be a day of rest!

Chipayas were experiencing freedom to try new things. Two believers now owned sewing machines; four typewriters were in use; Ceferino was president of Chipaya's first cooperative; and they built sheep dips to kill the ticks on their flocks. Ceferino and Zenobio even tried growing barley and wheat, but although the plants grew well, the heads of grain did not mature.

The Catholics purchased a battery-powered loud-speaker which they enjoyed using like a new toy. It ran on eight D-cells. They put the speakers up in the bell tower for the entire town to hear. On Sunday they broadcast songs and Bible messages, and on Tuesday morning at 6:30 they started announcing a town meeting for later that day.

At another long town meeting, Ron heard they might even have phone connections with Sabaya within a year. They already had poles, wire and one phone!

Some acquisitions were more useful than others: the Bolivian Minister of Agriculture gave them a big tractor which wasn't functioning. Ron wasn't sure they would use it since they didn't want to pay for gas or oil, but he tightened the bolts and asked our mission pilot to bring hydraulic fluid the next time he came.

Realizing we would be leaving before long, men bought some of our carpentry tools, tools for repairing bicycles, and even the Melodica. Several folks discovered they had musical ability. Our friend Mateo now played a trumpet by ear and was composing Christian hymns! We tried to explain music notation so he could play the Melodica, but one afternoon wasn't quite enough time! He had also taken a short mechanics course, expecting that someone in Chipaya might soon buy a truck.

They were also discovering new ways to share the Good News about God. Maximo and five others from the Catholic group bicycled through sand and rivers and against strong winds to preach in several Aymara villages during three one-week trips. This was like Samaritans witnessing to Jews. As in Jesus' day, some towns welcomed them while others didn't.

When the entire community met to discuss the use of the big (Catholic) church, Vicente, the shaman, grumbled, "The Catholics have no right to meet in *our* big church. It's for the idols and the pagans." An unbeliever demanded, "Why are you so strong against the Catholics? Where are you when people are chosen to host the fiestas? You don't help serve the idols and the demons, anyway. The fiesta responsibilities are too much for us now that we're only a few, whereas the Christians are many." And so the most powerful shaman was voted down and the Catholics continued to meet in their big church!

Later that week Maximo and other Catholic leaders held four days of classes before the priest came to baptize babies. The Chipayas asked Maximo, "Why aren't your children baptized?" He said, "I think it's better to wait till they're old enough to decide for themselves then let them be baptized to confirm their faith."

Director!

In February, 1975, Ron was appointed Acting Director for the work in Bolivia from June until conference in August. This meant that when school was out we would go to Tumi Chucua instead of Chipaya. Debbie groaned and Barbie cheered when they heard the news. Meanwhile, Ron tried to line up someone to check the translation with him in September.

But at conference in August our leaders asked him to please let his name be on the ballot for director. He said, "I'd much rather finish the Chipaya New Testament first." They said, "We need you now." So reluctantly he said, "Okay" and was elected director by almost all of the members. Suddenly the Chipaya translation came to a grinding halt. Thankfully the Chipaya believers were strong and growing.

So we stayed at Tumi. Besides relating to members and attending linguistic and other conferences, Ron's job as director included relating to government officials and whoever knocked on our screen door. One busy weekend we entertained a local lawyer, a Peruvian pastor, five Swiss-Bolivians, and four European tourists!

As Director, Ron had a lot of plates to keep spinning.

Government-Related Responsibilities

Being director meant visiting officials in La Paz and entertaining them when they visited Tumi. One day we fixed a fish and chip dinner for a couple of air force officials and our JAARS pilots. The next day Bolivian President Banzer, with his family and entourage, a total of eighteen, came for the weekend – unannounced, for safety reasons. The President liked being at Tumi and fishing in the lake. We had the privilege of cooking Sunday dinner for him and his family. He said, "My father taught me to love my country and my mother taught me to love God." We were thankful for a president sympathetic to the Gospel, and for the opportunity to translate the Bible in Bolivia.

The President's pilot on one visit was Colonel Salomon who had flown President Barrientos to Chipaya in 1965. Ron asked him, "Remember when you flew to Chipaya ten years ago?" He grinned and said, "I'll never forget that trip! The wind that made me stay overnight, and the frozen airplane motor in the morning! Do you still live up there?" Ron said, "Oh, yes, but a lot has changed since then."

Because of our government contract, various agencies requested linguistic articles, annual reports, museum artifacts and photographs, copies of things we printed, help with a bilingual school system, etc.

At the same time, one official questioned Ron about giving the Chipaya language to the CIA for World War use! It was amazing how that idea persisted! The anti-American sentiment was strong in academic circles.

One of Ron's first challenges was to write an eighteen-page paper in Spanish about what SIL was doing in Bolivia, and why, and present it at an anthropological conference in La Paz.

The atmosphere was hostile because many of the anthropologists present wanted missionaries thrown out of Bolivia. One item on the program was to view the film, *Vuelve Sebastiana* (Sebastiana Returns), which showed Chipayas sacrificing animals and barely eking out an existence from their barren land. After Ron presented his paper, he said, "The movie depicts the Chipayas as downtrodden, helpless, hopeless people, but they aren't at all like that. They are very much alive, intelligent, progressive and ambitious. They have the largest school in the area, own two sewing machines, a truck and…" Suddenly all the indigenous people present jumped to their feet, clapping and cheering. In an instant, the whole atmosphere changed, and the door swung wide open for friendly conversations about SIL's work!

Translation-Related Projects

At Tumi, I was typing Acts on the ITEL typewriter so we could print trial copies for the church leaders, but it went slowly because it was rough copy. Each key stroke on the ITEL punched a different combination of seven holes on a paper tape. The big advantage was that now corrections and changes could be made on the tape without retyping everything.

We took copies of Luke and Acts 1-16 to Ceferino and Maximo to edit. A big smile spread across Maximo's face as he started reading and he exclaimed, "It really sounds good! There are a few little things to correct, but it's *good*!" That was great news. If I kept pecking away, I should be able to retype the rest of the New Testament by the following August.

At the same time, a new Heidelberg offset press arrived in La Paz for CALL (Committee for Aymara Literacy and Literature) which in Spanish was called CALA. Aymara pastors at CALA produced and printed hundreds of Sunday school lessons and thousands of Aymara songbooks and tracts. We wondered if maybe now they would be able to print New Testaments. Our colleague, Fran MacNeill, was the CALA supervisor.

Meanwhile, the Chipayas kept asking, "Is our New Testament ready?" Our 1976 report was based on only three weeks in the village. We were hoping Ron would soon be free to resume checking the translation, but several colleagues asked him to please let his name stand again for director, and when he did he was elected for one more year.

When Ron flew to the highlands on group business in September he flew on to Chipaya for a couple days to tell the believers the New Testament would be delayed another year. He was glad to see that Maximo had already revised and corrected three-fourths of the New Testament.

At the same time, Ceferino said, "My daughter Victoria is pregnant and wants to get married and a lady in my group is very sick and will probably die soon. What does the Bible say about marriages and funerals?" Ron was glad for another chance to teach the believers.

Our Last Family Winter in Chipaya

When our girls finished their school year in June, 1976, we flew to Chipaya for eight days to encourage the believers.

We arrived just as the Chipaya school was being dismissed for winter vacation. The director and teachers were drunk. The director was saying, "Kick out the gringos! Smash down the churches with the tractor. Force the believers to drink. Don't let Florencio be a religion teacher. Don't let the girls braid their hair this way. Don't let the boys wear tunics to school. Make them talk Spanish!" Folks said he and Vicente, the head shaman, were buddies. Obviously there was still opposition to the believers and even to the Chipaya culture in general.

In spite of the director, the rest of the teachers seemed positive and one lady said, "The Chipayas speak well of you and have been waiting for you." That was encouraging.

On that visit, Debbie helped more Chipaya and Aymara children sew rag dolls, and all our girls enjoyed sliding on the ice once more.

When we worshiped with the Catholics in their big church we were glad to see they had white-washed all the blood splotches on the walls and floor. Our girls enjoyed the Catholic service best because they used the songbooks. The Spanish songs were easiest to read and the girls did quite well reading Chipaya but trying to read the Aymara songs was a challenge for all of us.

It was *cold* in the church that day – only 40 degrees! After sitting on the stone floor for two hours, we all had to thaw out in the sunshine! Debbie, Carla and Barbie all had their hair braided Chipaya style, and Debbie wore my Chipaya dress. The Chipaya ladies loved the girls' braids and said, "This is their town: they learned to walk here."

Each Sunday several people, including young people, entered God's Way. Some were even from families who a few years earlier would have disowned them for leaving the old ways. From the leaders' rosters, the Christian community numbered about 325 – almost a third of the Chipayas! What a joy!

We sold the last hymnbook the morning we left.

Chipaya-Related Activities

In September, after being elected director for one more year, Ron sandwiched in a two-day visit to Chipaya. He was relieved to find there was a new school director and Florencio had been teaching religion classes since July.

As usual, he took out Spanish Bibles and New Testaments, encouraging folks to read them until the Chipaya New Testament was printed. As a result, the Bible became their authority and Maximo even told the Catholic priest, "If anything doesn't agree with what I read in the Bible, I can't practice it or teach it."

Maximo told Ron, "In the teaching seminars, the Catholics prayed to Mary. We asked them, 'Does the Bible teach us to do that?' The priests answered, 'It's in other books written shortly after the Bible. It isn't making Mary to be God, but just remembering her as a very good woman who is close to Jesus.'"

On Sunday when Ron met with Ceferino's group, two new families entered God's Way. From after church till seven at night there was a constant stream of people, so he didn't even get a chance to eat.

In early December Ron, Amy and I spent a couple weeks in Chipaya. Amy enjoyed playing with other children. Since we didn't expect to spend much more time in Chipaya and the house now belonged to Maximo and his uncle, we continued selling our things.

When Ismael's father came to Chipaya he asked Ceferino, "How did your wife get well? I've been to all the shamans and sacrificed many animals, but my mother is no better." When Ceferino said, "The Lord healed her," Jose said, "Then please come and pray for my wife." Before Ceferino went, he and Ron looked up verses about praying for healing.

On Sunday Ron worshipped with about a hundred and fifty Catholics for two and a half hours in the morning. There were three good sermons on the Ten Commandments, Christ's condensation into two commandments, and on the New Commandment to love one another.

After the meeting, they played Aymara songs over the loudspeaker from the church tower, then when a group of believers arrived from Ayparavi in the afternoon, they all met for another two and a half hours and broadcast that whole meeting which was led by Tomas, our former shaman friend! The four ladies and four fellows on the worship team sang a lot of songs, including one Tomas had composed.

Tomas spoke from Colossians 3 about the Old Life and the New Life. It was amazing to hear him tell how evil and hatred had filled his heart when he was a major shaman, and how different life was now, and how we should live as Christians!

The Chipayas planned to host about 2000 Catholics from the whole area the following November. They had committees to plan the food, housing, bread making, meetings, etc. Each family was to provide one hundred pounds of food plus a sheep – a huge commitment for such poor people.

One night nine men and ladies recorded songs in our house. They practiced announcing the numbers about as much as they practiced the songs!

As usual, we look turns meeting with the three church groups. One Sunday we worshipped with eight men, six ladies and six children in Ceferino's small "Church of Ephesus." Though few, they had given sixty pesos to the Bolivian Bible Society. The group seemed to be growing with Feliciano as the new leader. Ceferino's daughter, Victoria, said, "Pray for my folks. They get mad at each other."

Another Sunday we met with Zenobio's group. Things seemed to be more stable.

As people began to realize we would be leaving in a few months, Maximo encouraged the believers to write more hymns so they could have a bigger hymnbook before we left. Ron asked Maximo, "What Bible teaching do we lack in the songs?" Then he and Maximo would choose a melody and compose a song on that topic. One of their favorite topics was about Jesus coming again. Maximo also challenged folks to read the Bible portions available. After church, twenty Catholics, including several teenage girls and young women, bought copies of 1 Corinthians, our newest publication.

Transformed People!

Over the years we watched many individuals choose to enter God's Way and welcome him into their lives. As we neared the end of our time in Chipaya, many folks came to tell us they had entered God's Way.

One morning years ago, Lorenzo had come to our house, his face streaked and his hair matted with blood. In a drunken fight with his own son, his son had stabbed him with a knife just below his eye. But now he had left that way of life and had destroyed two community idols that he was responsible for appeasing. Now only three big idols remained in East-Side!

When we met with Ceferino's group, his sister, Modesta, now a believer, was there with both her girls, Antoka and Victoria. She and her husband asked Maximo to bring a group of believers to Ayparavi to destroy their family idol and its altar.

We learned Aurelio, our shepherd boy, had died holding his Bible and little songbook. No one knew what sickness took him but now his mother had entered God's Way and treasured his Bible and songbook. She, too, asked the believers to destroy her family altar in front of the pagan church. The believers always prayed for God's protection before destroying an idol or an altar, since they knew how powerful the evil spirits could be.

One day a young mother with a baby on her back approached us in the plaza, smiling shyly, asking, "Do you know me?" I shook my head. "I'm Damiana, Maxine's daughter." No wonder I didn't recognize her: I had hardly seen her since those early days when her mom washed clothes with me.

One day a fellow came wanting carbon copies of a song he had written. He looked familiar so I asked, "What's your name?" He said, "Carlos." When I asked, "Remember how you used to be against the believers?" He said, "Yes! And I drank and fought all the time. Once I cut a lady's head open with a broken bottle, but Tall Brother cured her! Now my whole family follows God!"

A few days later a lady who came to buy medicine and a Bible asked Ron, "Do you know me?" When he said, "No," she pointed to a big scar on her forehead. "I'm Viviana, the lady Carlos clobbered with a jagged, broken bottle years ago! Remember?" "Oh yes!" With a big smile she added, "Now I've entered God's Way!" It all seemed too good to be true.

Then a young fellow asked, "Do you recognize me?" Again we had to say "No." He said, "I'm Jose. You bandaged my leg when I broke my bone! I've entered God's Way, too!" Our little friend Joey was now a handsome young man!

We were happy to hear that Justino, Grandpa Sunday's son, had entered God's Way in answer to his dad's last request.

One of our last days in Chipaya, a tiny little Grandma with a great big smile came to our house and said, "My sons built me a new house. Come see it," and she led Amy and me to the cutest little round house we had ever seen. It almost looked like a play house! She proudly announced, "Tomas and Santiago and Pedro made it just for me! They have all entered God's Way and I have, too." And to think that fifteen years ago no one seemed to care if the old folks lived or starved to death!

It was so beautiful and amazing to see changed lives. The long truck trips, the cold, windy days and nights, the headaches and long hours of work were nothing compared to this joy!

Unfortunately, there were some who still rejected God: Vicente the Shaman, for one.

Zenobio recalled, "When I first entered God's Way, Vicente came to my house ranting, 'Down with the believers! Down with Zenobio's church! Down with the Catholics! Down with Ceferino's church! My prayers are stronger than all of theirs! My rituals and witchcraft are stronger!'" Then Zenobio added, "Vicente still comes around and curses me, but I don't pay any attention to him."

Feliciano had also faced threats and persecution from the time he entered God's Way, and it still continued. He said, "Vicente has cursed me twice recently. Just last week he threatened, 'I'm going to kill you. I'm going to suck your blood. Then you'll die like Andres did.'" Feliciano and Ron talked for a long time about many things, reading from the Bible and praying. Since he could also read Aymara, Feliciano was starting to use the Aymara Sunday school materials published by CALA in La Paz.

Others, like Maximo Lopez, sometimes seemed close to entering God's Way but hadn't made the commitment yet.

Maximo Lopez was a friendly teenager when we first arrived in Chipaya. He is pictured in the *National Geographic* Magazine (November 1974) planting quinoa with his young son. Santusa, his wife, taught our girls to weave. Several times over the years he came to our house when drunk, saying, "I'm going to quit drinking. I really am, Tall Brother. I'm going to quit drinking and become a believer." We knew it was on his mind, and we hoped he would do it someday. Now he and Santusa bought a Bible, which was often the first public sign of interest in the Gospel.

6
THE CELEBRATION
1977-1978

FINAL CHECKING AND PRINTING

When Ron finished his second year as director in August, 1977, it was five years since our last furlough. Should we take a year's furlough now and finish the New Testament afterwards? Or should we finish the New Testament first then stay three years in the U.S. while Debbie, Carla and Barbie finished high school? We all voted to stay and finish.

That meant we had just one school year to finish and print the New Testament. There wasn't time to send it out of the country for printing – and no one in Bolivia had ever printed a New Testament so we had lots of questions. We asked Fran MacNeill, "Do you think CALA could print it?" Fran supervised the Aymara pastors in CALA, a print shop which produced songbooks and materials for Aymara congregations. We asked Fran, "Do you think you could get Bible paper? And could your presses handle it? Would CALA workers have time to do it with all their other jobs?" When Fran and the CALA team said, "Yes, we'll do it!" the Lord seemed to whisper, "Go for it!"

So when should we have the dedication? Easter Sunday? Why not? Easter was usually about mid-April. When we looked at a 1978 calendar, we groaned, "Oh no! Easter is on March 26!" Could we possibly have the New Testament checked, typed, printed and bound in seven months?

Fran MacNeill warned, "You'll need to send us the photo-ready pages in sections so we can start printing it, and we'll need the complete manuscript by the end of December." That gave us just four and a half months to get it photo-ready! The entire New Testament had been in first draft for over two years, but it all needed a final check. We took a deep breath, asked God to help us, and begged everyone to pray.

We asked the World Home Bible League (now The Bible League), "Would you underwrite the Chipaya New Testament?" They answered, "Gladly! We estimate that printing 800 copies will cost $8,000."

A few New Testament books had been printed earlier, so they were in good shape. Martha Garrard had recently retyped some books from Ron's rough drafts, and Karen Beachy, a young Mennonite lady, had also typed some books, so these were ready for the final edits. Other books still had multiple corrections and revisions scribbled in, which needed to be incorporated into a clean copy, before the final revision. After that the entire New Testament had to be retyped on the ITEL as this was still "B.C." – Before Computers!

To correlate our work with CALA, the Gospels had to be readied first. Ron decided to check one-third of the manuscript at a time so one section could be corrected and retyped while he checked the next one. He would check Section 1 (the Gospels) in September; Section 2 (Acts through Corinthians) in October-November; and Section 3 (the rest of the New Testament) in November-December.

Each checking trip took him from Tumi, at 600 feet altitude in the north eastern Amazon jungle, over the Andes at 17,000 feet to Chipaya at 12,000 feet in west central Bolivia. It would have been impossible without our JAARS pilots, the supercharged Cessna, and the help of another missionary pilot.

While Ron checked Section 1, I chose illustrations from the David C. Cook series, and suggested titles in Spanish.

Since Martha was now secretary for the new director, we needed other accurate typists. Bonnie Lyall, a short-term member, was excellent but couldn't do it alone. Karen Beachy had returned to Ohio but hadn't found another job yet, so by HAM radio we asked, "Would you consider returning to help type the Chipaya New Testament?" She answered, "I could come from October 10 till the end of the year." We said, "Please do!"

Checking Section 1

Mid-September, Ron flew to Cochabamba. A missionary pilot stationed in Cochabamba said, "I'll be flying to several highland villages on September 15. I have room for one more passenger, and could fly you to Chipaya if you like!"

Thankfully, Maximo was free to work and they checked Matthew, Mark and John. Luke had been revised previously, so now the Gospels were ready for final typing on the ITEL. While Ron revised Section 1 in Chipaya, Bonnie typed and I proofread Section 2.

The end of September, our JAARS pilot, Tom Hutson, flew to get Ron. He flew from Tumi to La Paz, then out to Chipaya, and back to La Paz with Ron. The next day, Thursday, Ron and Tom were to fly from La Paz to Tumi.

That morning, in the jungle, Bonnie said, "I just can't seem to get anywhere in typing Revelation. My back aches and my shoulders feel tired. I can't get comfortable on the chair. Even my clothes feel uncomfortable, and I can't concentrate. There is no sensible reason for any of these aggravations. The last time I felt this way was when I was pasting up the final pages of the Siriono New Testament."

It reminded us that "...we are not fighting against people... but against the evil rulers and authorities of the unseen world..." who didn't want the Chipayas to have God's Word in their own language. So we needed to "Use every piece of God's armor..." and "Pray at all times" (Eph. 6:12, 13, 18).

We were praying when the phone rang. Bobbie Deister, our radio operator, said, "Tom and Ron have left La Paz, heading north over the Andes, toward Tumi." A little later, she reported, "They can't get above the clouds. The plane is icing up and landmarks are obliterated." I called Ramey, Tom's wife, to pray. She said, "I've had a strange foreboding ever since Tom left on this flight. Verses I read talked about the Lord blessing 'you and your children,' and about the dead not being able to praise the Lord any longer on earth, but that 'we can.'" We cried as we begged God to keep our husbands safe.

A bit later Bobbie reported, "They're returning to La Paz." Thirty minutes later she reported, "They just landed safely in La Paz." We said, "Thank you, Lord!"

Later that afternoon, Bobbie reported, "Tom said the skies are clear so they're flying to Cochabamba and tomorrow they'll fly home." But a while later she called back saying, "As they crossed the last mountains and approached the Cochabamba valley, a violent storm blew in so they couldn't land. They're on their way back to La Paz." Ramey and I kneeled together again and cried and prayed for God to protect them. What if they didn't have enough fuel? What if clouds closed the high mountain passes? What if...? What if...? When Bobbie finally reported, "They're on the ground in La Paz," we wept for joy and relief.

We thanked the Lord for His protection – but the impression lingered. We were in a battle against all the evil powers who didn't want the Chipaya New Testament printed.

Early Friday morning, clear skies beckoned and the little Cessna finally carried Tom and Ron safely home.

Checking Section 2

In October, Bonnie and Karen typed the photo-ready copy of Matthew, Mark and John. Now Section 2 was ready to be revised in Chipaya. Since it was time to plant quinoa, we asked everyone to pray that Maximo would be free to work with us.

This time I flew to Chipaya with Ron. When we arrived at eight in the morning after our ninety-minute flight from Cochabamba, Maximo had the house open, and served us tasty quinoa soup. We saw quite a few people, sold medicine, etc., but couldn't check translation because both sides of town were building a string of classrooms by the plaza. We hoped Maximo's teen-age son could work in his place, but he was in Ayparavi helping his grandmother plant her quinoa. Maximo delayed planting his own crops to work with Ron. We asked the folks at Tumi to pray for someone to help check the translation.

Tuesday, Maximo was excused from town work – we never heard why, but thanked the Lord. They read through most of Luke one more time.

Wednesday, Maximo's wife, Vicenta, came to town with four-year-old Santiago, to work on the school in Maximo's place so they wouldn't be fined for not working. She carried large, heavy adobes and pails of mud or water for the working men. This freed Maximo to work all day, checking the rest of Luke and the first chapters of Acts. But the townspeople grumbled, "He shouldn't make his wife work while he sits and rests all day."

That afternoon Santiago and Rebeca, his four-year-old playmate, found matches and were playing near a pile of straw in their house. The inevitable happened. Neighbors tried to put out the flames while others ran to tell Vicenta, "Your little boy almost burned your house down!" She ran home, scared and crying. All the straw was burned up, as well as a little table, and some boards. Poor Vicenta was too upset to go back to work. She grabbed Santiago's hand and hurried back to their country home where she had left the three older children alone to watch the flocks.

Ron sent another message to Tumi, "While Maximo's wife was working in his place, their little boy almost burned down their town house, so there's no one to work in his place. Maximo also counsels church members and visits sick folks. Please pray for him and for someone to check the translation with me."

Thursday town work was called off, except for Wednesday's absentees, so Maximo was free to check Romans and 1 Corinthians. Florencio also worked a few days and Maximo stopped to check the last few chapters before going for straw. Just one more section to go!

Ron planned to return in December to check the last section of the New Testament. I told Maximo, "I'd come in December if we could have reading classes." He said, "They'll come to read if you serve bread like you did ten years ago!"

Unfortunately, it didn't work out to do that.

Checking Section 3

The first section – all four Gospels – was sent to CALA for printing the end of November. While I chose illustrations, Bonnie and Karen retyped the second section. Happily, this time Maximo and Feliciano were free to fly to Cochabamba to check the third section with Ron in the city. They were thrilled with the ninety-minute flight, pointing out all the familiar landmarks, marveling at the rugged mountains and finally at the beautiful green, Cochabamba valley.

Ron was glad to work in Cochabamba, out of the high altitude and free of interruptions. He ate meals in the mission house while Maximo and Feliciano chose to spend their food allowance at local stores and restaurants. When they finished checking the New Testament, Ron paid them for their work and gave them bus fare to Oruro and truck fare to Chipaya.

Beating the Deadline!

Back at Tumi, Ron proofread the second section for printing then gave the last section to the typists. As they typed it, he proofread it, so when they finished typing Revelation chapter 22 on December 29, he also finished the proofreading! Wow! It had taken four and a half months of concentrated work for everyone involved, but the Lord helped us beat the deadline by one day!

This called for a celebration, complete with speeches, flowers and a cake in the shape of an open Bible.

A gentleman from the U.S. happened to be visiting just then. We were standing around talking, enjoying cake and lemonade, when suddenly a loud explosion shook the wooden frame building. Everyone jumped and the visitor instinctively dove under a wooden bench for cover. When everyone started laughing, he sheepishly crawled out. We explained, "This is how we celebrate *very* special occasions!" He had just regained his composure when there was another explosion. This was obviously not his way of celebrating. After a long pause, a third explosion shook our building. Someone said, "That's it. Just three." Our visitor mumbled, "Thank goodness!"

Planning the Dedication

On January 5, despite its being the rainy season, Ron returned to Chipaya to help plan the dedication with about a dozen leaders from all the churches. They chose Maximo, from the Catholic Church, to be the main organizer; Feliciano, from Ceferino's church, as president; and Guzman, from Zenobio's church, as treasurer. Three ladies were to plan the meals.

They said, "The dedication should be in the plaza, using the Catholics' loud speaker. Let's start with the national anthem in Spanish and Chipaya, then each church group (three in Chipaya, one in Ayparavi and Zenobio's home church) will sing a song, read Scripture, and bring a message. Someone from CALA will also bring a message and Tall Brother will say a few words." They decided to take an offering to give to CALA for their ministry. Even Zenobio's group, who usually kept to themselves, seemed excited about taking part. The committee wrote out the programs for the morning and afternoon meetings with twenty-seven and twenty-four items, respectively, so Ron could have them printed in Cochabamba.

Evaluating Our Course

In January when Ron happened by Maximo's house at meal time, his wife seemed embarrassed as she handed him a bowl of quinoa soup, saying, "I know you have lots of good things to eat in Cochabamba." Maximo and Feliciano's time in Cochabamba had obviously increased the gap between us, as they felt the strangeness of an American world and saw all our cultural trappings.

As Ron considered that and other situations, he wrote: "The same is true of flying to Chipaya. Planes made life much more comfortable for us, and we could not have finished the New Testament in this time frame without them, but they may actually have hindered the work we came to do. We have lost the identification we had when we traveled by truck. Where is the balance?

"Fussing over the food rations from CARE was normal but disheartening. We could never please everyone; give-aways stimulated greed and jealousy. The same was true even in Bible times. After Jesus fed five thousand people, they resented him for not continuing free meals. Countries resent the U.S. even though we're more generous than anyone else. And don't we tend to be greedy when there's a limited supply of free items? Handouts tend to have value in proportion to the effort or money expended to gain them.

"The Catholics seem to be slipping back to drinking, following Florencio's example. He seems to be proud about being a teacher, yet it's the teachers who got him to drink again. I intended to help him by getting him the government salary to promote Chipaya reading and writing in the school, but maybe I did the wrong thing. Maybe we from developed countries tend to think that things and position are helpful and progressive, when sometimes they aren't.

"Zenobio's group likes the little New Testaments with Psalms, but they tend to use them as *patches* to draw out evils. All we can do is explain the truth and trust the Lord to help them leave these practices. At least they are looking to the Lord and His power rather than to the shamans.

"And could our presence be inhibiting? The church grew fastest when we weren't able to be there so much. We need to bring the initial vision and give them God's Word, but then it needs to be *their thing*. I'm afraid we didn't always make the right decision but I'm sure the Lord will continue to use his Word to build his church."

Printing Challenges

Meanwhile, the CALA printing team was facing their set of challenges. They had never printed a New Testament nor attempted to print on Bible paper. However, with the new Heidelberg Offset press, they didn't anticipate any serious problems.

But there were a few things they hadn't counted on. The packages of Bible paper were not all cut straight. Some of the paper had gotten damp in transit and refused to go thru the machine. In his eagerness to do a perfect job, Felix was reluctant to share the printing responsibilities. CALA's clients from eleven missions all seemed to need a rush job and Fran MacNeill, the general planner and manager, was in the U.S. for a month helping her parents.

Just then Martha Garrard needed emergency dental work, so she took her vacation and flew to La Paz, staying with Marion Heaslip, Fran's co-worker. Before going, Martha asked Ron, "Anything I can do to help?" He asked, "Could you check how the printing is coming along?" From CALA she sent him some sample pages, but couldn't find enough consecutive pages to assemble even one of the thirty-three sections, so her first job was to organize and chart all the printed pages.

After celebrating the half-way mark, the print shop staff discovered they had only printed a quarter of the New Testament. By checking off each printed sheet, however, they soon knew exactly which pages they needed in order to complete a section.

But they weren't home free yet. Twice the triple-strength plate glass, which they used for exposing the printing plates, exploded mysteriously. Then the folding machine wrinkled several hundred large printed sheets. After that, Martha and Marion helped the print shop staff and other guests and friends fold all the New Testament pages by hand. Later, a surge of power followed by a partial black-out silenced the press. Felix was sure it was burned out but the CALA staff radioed everyone at Tumi to please pray and before long someone located a circuit breaker – something Felix had never heard of – and soon the press was humming again.

Although prospects often looked dim, the CALA workers poured heart and soul into printing, folding, assembling, sewing and binding the New Testaments. They often worked evenings, weekends and holidays; and when there was a transportation strike, they walked to work, which for some meant miles. The final touch was printing a series of colored pictures for inside the front and back covers. The ones in front pictured highlights of Jesus' life while those in the back featured Palestinian culture and activities. Another special feature was a map of the Chipaya area drawn to the same scale as the map of Palestine so they could see that walking from Chipaya to Ayparavi was like walking from Jerusalem to Jericho. The dust cover pictured a small llama in a green pasture with verses about Jesus the Good Shepherd. The finished product was beautiful!

Other Challenges

Meanwhile, the JAARS pilots and mechanics at Tumi were facing their own set of challenges. As Easter approached, the Cessna 206, which we needed to fly people and New Testaments to Chipaya for the dedication, developed a problem that baffled them for days -- but they were finally able to solve it.

We wished we could have invited the entire CALA staff and others to meet the Chipaya believers and celebrate with them, but Ron was keeping the list of outsiders short. Co-workers would have liked to document the celebration to share with friends in the U.S., but Ron said, "I'm sorry. The Chipayas don't like pictures. It would spoil the day for them and this has to be *their* day, not ours." It would have made a picturesque movie, but the price was too high.

Gathering for the Celebration

Our family and Bonnie, who had helped type the New Testament, flew to Chipaya on Wednesday before Easter. It was fun listening to our girls tell Bonnie about all their fun times in Chipaya: playing in the sand, playing moonlight shadow tag, and learning to weave.

Saturday morning Fran MacNeill arrived by Jeep with three CALA workers, bringing 198 New Testaments, Aymara literature and an accordion, guitar and violin. That afternoon the CALA pastors sang and preached in the plaza with a loudspeaker as crowds of Chipayas and visiting Aymaras listened.

Saturday evening Florencio served supper to our family and the CALA folk. Then we visited the three churches in town, which were all holding special meetings. The CALA fellows sang, presented CALA materials, gave a short message, and encouraged the Chipayas in each church to read their New Testament.

Sunday morning Guzman served us bread and hot tea, specialty foods in Chipaya. Quinoa soup with chunks of meat and piles of fluffy quinoa had been cooking in half barrels over open fires since daybreak.

Soon our JAARS pilot, Tom Hutson, flew in bringing our director, Dave Farah, the head of the Bolivian Bible Society, and the New Testaments. Then the long-awaited Celebration began!

* * * * *

God of the Impossible

The little village of Chipaya has witnessed countless processions honoring evil spirits. Flutes, drums, and panpipes have repeated the same snatches of tunes through long, freezing nights as men and women have danced and drunk, afraid to stop lest they offend the merciless spirits.

The Chipayas have held tenaciously to their isolated way of life, their language, their ancient dress and hair style, their round clay homes, but most of all to their ways of worship. Life has revolved around the sacrifices and rituals, which have bound them to this desolate plateau between ranges of the Andes.

But today, Easter Sunday, I was marching with 250 Chipayas in the first Christian parade. Impossible! – But true! It was a beautiful sight: two long columns of men in brown and white pin-striped tunics flanking a column of women in dark homespun dresses, hair braided meticulously.

It was a march of triumph, but victory had not come easily. When the first few entered God's Way the community tried to banish them, saying, "If you follow God you are not Chipayas." But they chose to endure robbery, slander and assault rather than abandon God.

It seems like yesterday that they blamed Ron and me for the flood which ruined their crops and toppled their homes. They cursed us with blood sacrifices, and then watched intently to see what would happen – but God intervened. The man who sprinkled the blood on our floor that day was marching today, transformed by the blood of Christ!

When the first eager Christians tried to have a meeting in this very plaza, Vicente, the chief shaman, incited his followers to beat them, tear their clothes and chase them out of town. He had long held undisputed control because of his great words and evil power, but today he stood on the sidelines alone, helplessly watching and listening to his former subjects sing "Glory! Hallelujah! The Church of God is moving onward!"

I could see Ron up front, dressed like the other men, but standing taller. He was their *Big Brother*, who for sixteen years has put their needs and wants before his own. He has been doctor, fix-it-man, and friend, introducing them to Christ and teaching them His Word. Today he would give them God's Word in their own language, clearly printed so they could read and study if for themselves.

Our four girls were somewhere in the crowd, too – our girls, who had made tunnels in this sandy soil; skated on the frozen river, had their long blond hair braided into a hundred tiny braids, Chipaya style, and had sung God's praises with them in three languages. Our girls, who had come to Chipaya as babies, were now young ladies.

The singing continued in Spanish until Tomas said, "That's enough Spanish. Let's sing in our own language!" This was the same Tomas who, years ago as a shaman, had cursed our plane so we would crash.

Feliciano sang heartily – Feliciano, who had proudly led so many drunken processions, carrying the head of the ram which had been sacrificed to the spirits.

And there was Ceferino, the first Christian, who stood alone for two years before anyone dared join him.

Familiar faces in the long columns brought a flood of memories. There was Carlos, the fiesta drummer, and Viviana, whose head he had split open with a broken bottle. Mateo; the mischievous little neighbor boy, who grew up to help translate God's Word. Sabina, who often feared for her little Rebeca's life after losing five other daughters. Zenobio, who had sacrificed fifteen sheep for his son's life, only to have him die the next day. Then, there were so many more that I didn't even know – everyone with a story of how God has snatched him from the clutches of the evil one.

Though my eyes blurred and I choked up, my heart kept singing "Glory! Hallelujah!" Just a few years ago Chipaya hearts seemed so hard and dry, but God had done the impossible.

Just then Bonnie whispered, "It's so impressive to me, I can imagine how you feel!" Then my thoughts turned to last fall. The New Testament manuscript had been set aside for two years while Ron directed the Wycliffe work in Bolivia, but the Chipayas wanted their New Testament *right now*. It still needed to be typed, checked again with the believers, retyped, printed, and bound – all in less than seven months if we were to give it to them before furlough. It had been almost six years since our last furlough. We weren't sure how soon we'd return to Bolivia, either, because Debbie, Carla and Barbie would be finishing high school. And the Chipayas were talking about leaving this desolate area.

It was now or never, so we set Easter as the dedication date, though it seemed ridiculously impossible. When short-term typist Karen Beachy said she would return to Bolivia to help Bonnie with the final typing, it was like God whispering, "Go ahead!"

Then we all started praying and working hard. Three times before Christmas Ron flew from our Tumi Chucua Center, near sea level, to Chipaya, at 12,000 feet. When Maximo spent almost full-time checking with him, we were sure God was saying "Yes!" Never before had Ron had consistent help in the village.

In September Ron checked the Gospels so Karen and Bonnie could start the final typing while he returned to Chipaya to check the rest. Then he proofread the Gospels so they could go to the printers. Deadlines. Impossible deadlines. But God helped us meet them. Checking, typing, and proofreading were all finished before New Year's. But could 200 copies be printed and bound before Easter, when no one had ever printed a New Testament in Bolivia before?

The challenge was accepted by Fran MacNeill and the CALL (CALA) staff of Aymara Christians. They had printed over a million pieces of literature, but never a New Testament. The paper arrived cut crooked. They were inexperienced with the Heidelberg press. The folding machine wrinkled the thin paper, so every page had to be folded by hand. Other jobs kept pressing in. Each set-back called for urgent prayer.

Martha Garrard spent her vacation in La Paz folding pages and charting progress. Even while Fran was gone for a month everyone worked faithfully. And they did a beautiful job! By Easter, they had 198 of the 600 copies ready to sell. Today Fran and the three pastor-printers felt well repaid for their hard work as they led the joyful procession with accordion, guitar, and violin.

God had done the impossible again.

Other visitors included Bolivia director, Dave Farah, pilot Tom Hutson, and Jaime Goytia of the Bolivian Bible Society. Dave had helped us settle in Chipaya the very first time and had helped many Chipayas find their way around the capital, La Paz. A few Aymaras from neighboring towns were also present.

Town officials joined us for flag raising and singing the national anthem in Spanish and Chipaya. Then after prayer, we all marched to the schoolyard for the program.

Chairs and plank benches lined the adobe platform, with a pulpit on one side and a display table for the New Testaments on the other. A row of New Testaments standing up looked like a parade of little white llamas.

Guests were thankful for the patchwork canopy of flour sacks that protected them from the brilliant sun. Some of us sat on the two benches facing the platform, but most of the 300 or 400 Chipayas preferred the ground. Our daughter, Amy, squeezed into the narrow shade of the school building with a line of mothers and small children.

As Maximo announced the first numbers on the program we wondered if all five churches would participate. They had never cooperated in anything before, and two groups had been told to attend a counter-program in another village. The printed programs included them all, but would they really take part? And if they didn't, would they buy and read the New Testament? We had tried to involve them all in the translation work and had taken turns meeting with them on Sundays. But to forget their differences and worship together – was it too much to expect? We scanned the crowd expectantly, fearfully.

But many people had been praying, and this was God's day.

One by one, as each congregation was called, the believers crowded onto the platform to sing their special songs, some accompanying themselves with flutes, drums and symbols. One choir wore red, yellow and green ribbons (like the Bolivian flag) tucked in their belts and draped over one shoulder. Each pastor gave a mini message, most of them reading from the brand new volumes. It was unbelievable! God had done it again!

Tomas, true to form, preached on the power of God. Florencio, who helped with the first draft of the New Testament, said, "This, God's Word, is very precious. It's really heavy – not to be taken lightly."

The CALA pastors said, "The Aymara New Testament is the one *we* love, though we do understand Spanish: Now here is your very own..."

The town mayor, not yet a believer, said, "You've left this Book as a flower in Chipaya." This was especially meaningful as no flowers grow in Chipaya's salty soil.

In their eagerness to receive their New Testaments, the translation helpers squeezed between or jumped over the row of little children who lined the platform. Besides ten copies given to individuals, seventy others were sold before the day ended. Thanks to the Canadian Home Bible League, we could sell them for an affordable $1.25 instead of the $9.33 it cost to print them.

Gregoria, one of the first women to buy her copy, admitted, "I can't read, but my son will read to me."

Tricolor ribbon bookmarks saying "YOOZ TAKU LIILAY = CHIPAYA = 1978" (God's Word Let's read) were pinned on those who bought Bibles.

After serving a dinner of quinoa, mutton, and corn to the whole community, the believers met for another program that lasted till nearly sundown. Maximo's closing prayer, like Solomon's prayer at the dedication of the temple, was a perfect climax to this overwhelming day. A few years, months, or even hours before, it seemed so impossible. But God had done it!

The next day we heard the old kind of music. It was the shaman, Vicente, with a cassette player tucked under his arm! Maybe one day even he will march in a Christian parade. Impossible? God loves to do the impossible![7]

Bread for Reading, II

On Monday life gradually got back to normal. Tuesday evening we started Chipaya reading classes in Zenobio's church by kerosene lamplight, for those who could already read Spanish. There wasn't time to teach those who couldn't read at all. We had come full circle, offering homemade bread for those who came to read – just like we did for the first nucleus of believers ten or twelve years earlier!

Ron and Maximo worked with the men on the right side of the church and I with the ladies on the left side, moving the benches around a bit. When their babies fell asleep, the mothers bundled them up and laid them on the floor as they did at home. They each read at their own rate, out loud, though not usually very loud. One little grandma was delighted when she could match words that looked alike!

Several men finished reading all five primers then Ron told them to look up a Scripture portion and read it in unison, to help each other with unfamiliar words. They read 1 Corinthians 13 about love, the Lord's Prayer, The Beatitudes, John 10 about the Good Shepherd, and John 14 about the way to heaven. At the end of each session we put the primers away and read a Bible story together then we'd say, "Come back tomorrow night," and give them each a couple pieces of bread for the walk home.

I spent the first week making bread, since it took all day to bake eight loaves in my tiny box oven. When classes grew from twenty to one hundred ten, Guzman had to take over, using his large round outdoor oven! We encouraged the church leaders to continue reading programs, suggesting Sundays after church since they were already all together.

We had introduced them to God and given them God's Word. At least a third of them had chosen to enter God's Way, and were reaching out to their families and townsmen. We could leave them now in God's hands. Our hearts were singing, "Glory, Hallelujah!"

God had come and was transforming their town!

7
LIFE IN CHIPAYA
BECAUSE GOD CAME

*After talking with Maximo recently,
I think this is what he would like to tell Ron...*

July, 2009
Dear Tall Brother,

It's been many years since I last wrote to you. I know you are in God's Town now – along with Florencio and Domingo and Roberto – so you won't get this letter, but I'd like to tell you about Chipaya, anyway.

When you first came to Chipaya [in 1961], all of us, except Ceferino, were worshipping the idols and evil spirits. We were proud about being independent and "free," but we didn't realize we were slaves to the evil spirits.

Remember when my baby son Demetrio was so sick? The shaman said, "Your parents are demanding that you sacrifice a white llama to them or they will eat your son's spirit and he will die." I got very angry because my parents had left me orphaned when I was small, and they surely knew I was much too poor to buy a white llama for a sacrifice. Then Ceferino said, "Go see Tall Brother. He has good medicine." When I visited you, you told me about a God who loved me and was stronger than the spirits. My wife and I decided to enter God's Way. Demetrio got better but later, when you were away, he got sick again and everyone said, "He will die unless you sacrifice to the spirits." But I said, "We have committed our lives to God and we will follow Him even if our baby dies." Then God healed him.

Before you learned our words, you brought a machine that told stories in our language [Gospel Recording records]. Our favorite story was about a lost sheep because we all knew about losing sheep. It said we were lost sheep and God was the Good Shepherd who was looking for us. Several of us borrowed the machine and secretly listened to the stories in our country homes at night. That way we learned about God without our families getting angry at us.

As you learned our language, you wrote it down and made reading books for us. It was hard to read because our words need many letters that aren't in the Spanish alphabet. You brought something new to read almost every time you came back to our village. We liked the songbooks and Bible stories best – especially the story about Elijah and the Prophets of Baal. We had reading classes, too, but the songbook was best for people to practice reading. Then you read sections of God's Word and sang songs on tapes. My wife liked to listen to the tapes because she never learned to read well. None of the women had been to school in those days. We finally got the Chipaya New Testaments on Easter Sunday in 1978.

Now all the boys and girls go to school. Remember when there were only five or ten children in school? Now we have the largest school in the whole area, all the way through high school! Of course it's in Spanish, but that means the young people can understand the Spanish Bible better.

There are many Aymara believers in the towns surrounding us. Of course most of us know some Aymara because we've always traded with them. They used to be our enemies, but not anymore. They visit our churches, and we visit theirs. They have a songbook with a lot of original songs. Their language was hard to read at first, but their tunes are easier to sing. Some of the Chipaya believers have translated their songs and even composed new ones. Then we type copies on the typewriters you left, and teach the new songs in church.

Some of our young men have even attended universities, and taken linguistic courses. Their teacher encouraged them to change our alphabet to be more like the Aymara alphabet, and less like Spanish. I don't like the new alphabet. It's different and it's harder to read, but the young men convinced the community to accept it.

We were out of Chipaya New Testaments for several years. Many families didn't have a single copy. We hoped you could come back and reprint the New Testament and translate the Old Testament, but you were busy giving God's Word to others who didn't have it in their language – then you got sick and died [in 2003].

Finally the young men traveled to the city of Cochabamba to ask the Bible Society to print more New Testaments for us. The Bible Society said, "Okay, but it should be revised first because it was translated long time ago." The young men wanted it to sound more like the Spanish Bible, so the Bible Society helped them revise the New Testament and type it on computers in the new alphabet.

Then of course we needed to teach people to read the new alphabet. We were glad that your wife came back and helped write new reading books [in 2004]. She also helped the Bible Society print our songbook in both alphabets. When the reading books were printed, we asked the Aymara school teachers to let us teach the Chipaya children to read and write in their own language, but they never let us do it. So the New Testament [revised and printed in 2005] isn't being used as much as it should be.

There is one more piece of good news: Some Christians in your country [Faith Comes by Hearing] are going to record our whole New Testament, so we can listen for half an hour each week then discuss what we have heard. That will help all of us understand God's Word better, and learn how to live more like God's children. To record it, many of us need to read well, so we can read what Jesus, Paul, Peter or Mary said. I guess I'd better start reading the new alphabet after all.

We still miss you, Tall Brother. Thank you for coming to bring us God's Word. We wish you could have stayed longer. Very few Chipayas worship and sacrifice to the spirits. The children don't even know what it was like when we all worshipped the spirits and got so drunk and had so many fights.

Many things are different. Most Chipayas wear bought clothes, and the women and girls don't braid their hair like they used to. Most houses are square with aluminum roofs. But the biggest and best change is that almost everyone has entered God's Way.

I'm almost seventy-five years old now, Tall Brother, so maybe I will join you soon. Until then, may God help us be faithful to Him and love each other.

Your Brother,
Maximo[8]

ENDNOTES

[1] *In Other Words,* February 1980, published by Wycliffe Bible Translators. Used by permission.

[2] Printed first in the December 25, 1966 issue of *Today,* a Sunday take-home paper published by Harvest Publications. Used by permission.

[3] Ronald D. Olson, "Mayan affinities with Chipaya of Bolivia I: Correspondences," 1964.
Ronald D. Olson, "Mayan affinities with Chipaya of Bolivia II: Cognates," 1965.

[4] Ronald D. Olson, "The Spire" Summer-Autumn 1974, Volume XXVI, Number 2. Published by Princeton Theological Seminary, Princeton, New Jersey 08540. Used by permission.

[5] *Translation Magazine,* October-November 1974, published by Wycliffe Bible Translators. Used by permission.

[6] *In Other Words,* November 1976, published by Wycliffe Bible Translators. Used by permission.

[7] *In Other Words,* Summer Edition, 1978, published by Wycliffe Bible Translators. Used by permission.

[8] First electronic rights: 2009, David C. Cook, Colorado Springs, CO 80918, USA.
http://www.davidccook.com. Used by permission.

**Intermedia
Publishing Group**

Publishing That Works For You

Do you need a speaker?

Do you want Fran Halterman to speak to your group or event? Then contact Larry Davis at: (623) 337-8710 or email: ldavis@intermediapr.com or use the contact form at: www.intermediapr.com.

Whether you want to purchase bulk copies of *When God Came to Town* or buy another book for a friend, get it now at: www.imprbooks.com.

If you have a book that you would like to publish, contact Terry Whalin, Publisher, at Intermedia Publishing Group, (623) 337-8710 or email: twhalin@intermediapub.com or use the contact form at: www.intermediapub.com.